*

DO YOU KNOW WHAT IT MEANS
TO MISS NEW ORLEANS?

DO YOU KNOW WHAT IT MEANS
TO MISS NEW ORLEANS?

A collection of stories & essays set in the Big Easy.

AN AROUSING ASSORTMENT OF TALES FILLED TO THE BRIM WITH BLOOD AND SPIT. FOLLOW OUR HEROES AND HEROINES AS THEY **ESCAPE FROM A SINKING CITY.** FEATURING: A WOMAN ON A FLYING TRAPEZE, A DOWN-AND-OUT JAZZ PIANIST, A TEENAGE FLOAT GRUNT, ACCLAIMED WRITERS, DRUNKEN PROFESSORS & RADICAL SOUTHERN INTELLECTUALS. CONTAINING AN ILLUSTRATED MAP OF THE HIGHEST ARTISTIC STANDARDS, MOUTHWATERING RECIPES & OLD ENGRAVINGS OF THE CRESCENT CITY THAT WERE DISCOVERED IN THE DEPTHS OF A LIBRARY IN THE ORIENT. **DO YOU KNOW WHAT IT MEANS?** MOURN THE CITY'S LOSS, FIGHT FOR ITS SURVIVAL AND CELEBRATE ITS LEGACY. THEN JOIN US, THE CELEBRATED AND ONLY WORLD-RENOWNED CHIN MUSIC PRESS, IN THE STREETS FOR MARDI GRAS.

fall 2012

a **BROKEN LEVEE BOOKS** *edition*

CHIN MUSIC PRESS — *PUBLISHERS*

SEATTLE

CHIN MUSIC PRESS INC.
2621 24th Ave. w.
Seattle, WA 98199
USA

http://www.chinmusicpress.com

Third edition [3]
Interior design: Craig Mod
Cover design: Josh Powell/Palindrome
Printed in CANADA by
Imprimerie Gauvin

DO YOU KNOW WHAT IT MEANS TO MISS NEW ORLEANS? (Well, do you?)

13-digit ISBN 978-0-9850416-0-1
2 3 5 7 11 13 17 19 23 29 31 37 41 43 47 53 59 61 67 71 (0)

"We're Getting Out of Here" by John Gravois was reprinted with permission from *The Chronicle of Higher Education*, copyright 2005.

We're especially indebted to the following publications, organizations and people: *Historical Sketch Book and Guide to New Orleans*, published in 1885 by New Orleans Press. We have reproduced some of the book's engravings and song lyrics. *The World from Jackson Square*, edited by Etolia S. Basso and published in 1948 by Farrar, Straus & Co. for excerpts from Sister Madeleine Hachard, Charles Lyell, Mark Twain and Walt Whitman. The Houston Institute of Culture for providing the transcript of Edward R. Murrow's interview of Louis Armstrong on its website. Finally, and most sincerely, we thank Eddie DeLange and Louis Alter for writing such a great song.

I know I'm not wrong
The feeling's getting stronger
The longer I stay away

✳

We want our city. And we don't want it to come back like no Disneyland for adults. It was getting that way anyway. We don't want that. Just give us a chance to collect ourselves.

— WYNTON MARSALIS
as quoted in *Rolling Stone*

Contents.

ALTERNATIVE* READING ORDER.

Inspired by the many different versions of the song
"Do You Know What It Means to Miss New Orleans?"

* It's not easy reliving the horrors of Katrina, especially if your home is in the Gulf Coast region. With that in mind, we have created an alternative table of contents that pays tribute to the many different renditions of "Do You Know What It Means to Miss New Orleans?" We played the different versions, thought about which stories related best, and reshuffled the book in a way that spreads the pain and the laughs.

*

Preface.

THIS BOOK SHOULD BEGIN with a certain musical phrase — best expressed on the trumpet — that every New Orleanian knows. It is that four-note announcement, with powerful emphasis on the third note — da-da-*DAAAAA*-da. The Mardi Gras call to arms, call to attention, call to parade. It is a phrase that wakes up the neighborhood and clears the air for a multicolored, umbrella twirling, brass-band swinging, shouting and stomping impromptu second line headed straight down the nearest street. It is a sound of home that I miss.

Even the mournful stories of this collection should be introduced with this phrase. The music of New Orleans — like the city itself — is able to move from mood to mood in ways that might surprise people from other cultures. The sense of loss is an inevitable theme of this book. Loss almost defines New Orleans at this time. But humor and beauty exist comfortably in these same pages. For those who do not already know, humor, beauty and the blues all live right alongside each other. Even after Katrina, laughter is the best life raft.

Of course New Orleans will be rebuilt, but it would be better off without that passive construction: New Orleans will rebuild. The people of this city are necessary for bringing this city back to some semblance of what it was. I say "of course" the city will return, but as I write, the fate of the Ninth Ward is still being debated. How much of this city will be lost? How much of the culture will fall to the force of this hurricane? How much of the culture will fall to the rebuilding process?

When President Bush stood on a disaster site in the neighboring state of Mississippi and declared that Senator Trent Lott's house would rise up again, bigger and better than ever, it made a few people shudder. Somehow this statement conveyed an image of Trent Lott's huge house standing on that spot while the surrounding land remained a disaster. George and Trent could sip their mint juleps on a spacious new veranda while the rest of the people still sat in a landscape of rubble waiting for a sip of water. That seems to be the vision that some have of this rebuilding process.

We should use that musical phrase to lead the people who are bringing this city back to life. Some of the current brass bands have names that are appropriate for this period — The Rebirth Brass Band, The New Birth Brass Band. Every nail that is pounded in this rebuilding process should be pounded with the sound of a brass band in the background. Or a zydeco band, or some New Orleans jazz. This will help those visitors who have come to aid in the reconstruction of New Orleans — and some of those visitors are necessary now — to keep it New Orleans. This will also help the locals remember what they are rebuilding. It is not just a city, not just houses — it is a culture.

New Orleans needs to beware of charity. In a place so desperate for help, some economic forces may step in with aid and entrench themselves in places where they would never before have been welcome. C.W. Cannon's piece, "The New Orleans Manifesto," shows that seemingly progressive economics was a threat to the city even before Katrina. If there is a Starbucks in the French Quarter, something has been lost. If there is a Mardi Gras parade sponsored by Pepsi, something has been lost. If the houses are being designed by Halliburton ... some things have already been lost.

Insert tuba solo here.

New Orleans culture is a thing of the past, and the past is a pretty good place to look when the present offers so little. At the same time, we do not want New Orleans to become a museum — or a caricature — of its past. We do not want New Orleans-land.

New Orleanians know that a culture is not just something that you look at or something you eat. In this city, culture is something you live. Culture is something you cook or build or sing. Yes, you can eat it, but it is better if you have a whole party around the act of eating. Personally, I am not a fan of crawfish, but I can enjoy a crawfish boil. Culture here is participatory. This is why the recipes found in our "Home Cooking" chapter so often involve large groups. This is why Mardi Gras is so successful, as Ray Shea's "I Was a Teenage Float Grunt" — in an odd way — illustrates. This is why we were able to get these writers — so many of them unknown — to contribute to this book.

Much of *Do You Know What It Means To Miss New Orleans?* looks to the culture as it was before this hurricane. These stories and essays do not look to the culture with a blind eye. The writers are no tourists. These essays will surprise the non-New Orleanian with their honesty. They will also surprise the New Orleanian with what they have to say about life pre-Katrina. Wait until you read Sarah Inman's story.

The voices of this book come with a sense of urgency, a necessity to get the story out. Many of the stories are about survival. Literal survival, as in Bill Lavender's escape from a sinking city, or cultural survival, as in Dar Wolnik's tribute to the farmers' market. These voices demand to be heard. Toni McGee Causey's extraordinary essay, "Where Grace Lives," will move anyone who has a heart. But, once again, this book is not all intensity and loss. Rex Noone's story — this book's lagniappe, a New Orleans thing — punctuates these pages with some humor. Together, these disparate works complete a portrait of New Orleans, not a complete portrait, but a true and unique one.

The bottom line is that we all want to keep this culture. If we could reverse the clock, we would see rooftops pushing up out of the black water, levees pulling all of that excess water to the sides and a city — New Orleans — drying off and rising to life. We need to keep in mind that this magic reversal of time is not possible. New Orleans will not be the same. The word "rebuilding" may give the wrong idea. Post-Katrina New Orleans will be new, and the odds are that it will not be better, unless the people return with a will to keep the character and culture of this city. What comes down from DC may be needed, but it is not New Orleans.

We do not know how much of New Orleans we will miss permanently, how much is gone, but we do know that a great culture was here once. We will need a good amount of Ms. Causey's grace to create it again. Studs Terkel wrote, "Hope has never trickled down. It has always sprung up." The same can be said for a culture.

Let that trumpet sound.

David Rutledge
October 2005

PÈRE ANTOINE'S DATE PALM

We play those dirges, and we have stuff that's
about death, and you learn to play those types
of songs. I know when I was growing up the
older people would say, "You've got to wait, boy."
Because when you leave space, the emotions set in.
When you play a dirge, you got to wait … When
you wait you can feel the power, that pathos.

— WYNTON MARSALIS

THE DIRGE

Just a closer walk with Thee
Grant it, Jesus, is my plea,
Daily walking close to Thee,
Let it be, dear Lord, let it be.

Crescent City.

HISTORICAL POPULATION STATISTICS

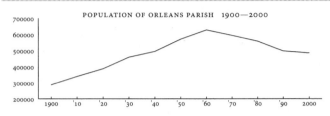

POPULATION OF ORLEANS PARISH 1900—2000

CENSUS DATA 1900

population:	287,104
white:	72.8%
african american:	27.1%
hispanic / latino:	n/a
asian:	0.2%

CENSUS DATA 2000

population:	462,269
white:	28.1%
african american:	67.3%
hispanic / latino:	3.1%
asian:	2.3%

MAP REFERENCE

VARIOUS MAPS & LOCATORS

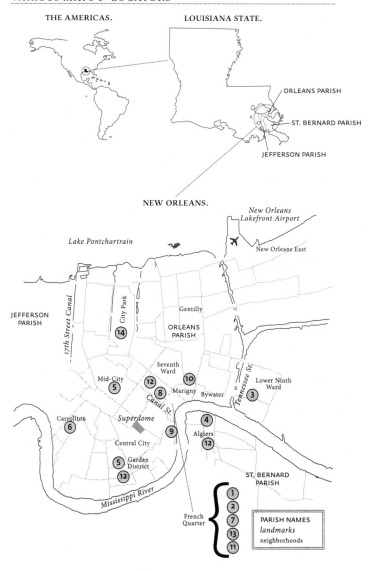

THE AMERICAS.

LOUISIANA STATE.

ORLEANS PARISH

ST. BERNARD PARISH

JEFFERSON PARISH

NEW ORLEANS.

New Orleans
Lakefront Airport

New Orleans East

Lake Pontchartrain

JEFFERSON
PARISH

City Park

Gentilly

ORLEANS
PARISH

Seventh
Ward

Mid-City

Marigny

Bywater

Lower Ninth
Ward

Carrollton

Superdome

Central City

Algiers

Garden
District

ST. BERNARD
PARISH

Mississippi River

French
Quarter

PARISH NAMES
landmarks
neighborhoods

Corners of the Quarter.

DAVID RUTLEDGE

THE ATM WOULD NOT GIVE ME MONEY. There was another bank one block away, and I turned down Chartres, passing the Napoleon House on the corner—a quirky little place with a four-seat bar near the front, good food, little tables, plus some nooks and rooms that added to the historic feel. I recall sitting in the courtyard, having lunch with my father, when a tropical rain began to plunk onto our table. The waiter moved the table under cover. The rain came so quickly and puddled so suddenly, that the water looked like it might overflow the courtyard. We watched the rain pouring straight down for about twenty minutes, while my dad—at seventy—had the first muffuletta of his life. When the rain was finished, we paid up, stepped outside and saw that the whole purpose of this downpour was to make New Orleans sparkle.

The next ATM would not give me money. Maybe it was already out. I may have waited too long; this was Saturday and many people had left. I was hoping to have some cash for any unexpected twists to this weekend, but I could still go to the store and buy some supplies by credit card.

At the end of the next block I turned the corner by Jackson Square. The place was much emptier than usual, but not yet

HAUNTED HOUSE ROYAL ST.

desolate. Some politicians have been trying to empty this square of its contents for the past few years, removing Tarot readers and their tables, palm readers, homeless and other characters. They thought that these moves would make the square more elegant, more appealing to tourists. This did not make the square more elegant; it only made it more empty. Luckily, on most days, magicians and fortune tellers still take their place. Various characters still bring the square to life. There is also a church.

On this day there was no music playing. Those social reformers have even tried to control the music, but now the musicians were missing for a different reason. Jackson Square has so much less soul without someone puffing on an old tuba, someone singing with all his gruff lung power from a park bench, maybe someone wearing a worn Phillies shirt playing a guitar. Ragtag and energetic, the spirit of New Orleans music. Crowds would gather around and feel the lifeblood of this culture—flowing for free, flowing from the street—through old brass instruments and patched up strings. When the music was in full swing, on my way to the bank or elsewhere, I would sometimes sit with the tourists, enjoying the sense of a city that has created a music unique to itself.

There was an A&P on the next corner, on Royal. It was usually open twenty-four hours, but a sign said that they were going to close at ten. The air conditioning was an overwhelming welcome as I stepped in from the humid street. The lines were not as long as they were last year for Ivan. Bananas. The aisles were so small that two people could not comfortably pass. Cans of tuna fish. Somehow they had crammed as much of a market as they could onto this corner of the Quarter. I bought milk, thinking that the power might stay on and that I could survive on cereal for a few days. It couldn't be more than a few days.

As I walked back to my apartment, carrying the bags and dripping in this evening heat, I passed some places already boarded up, businesses shut down. People who didn't seem at home with tools were now having to take out their drills and hammers. This shutting down of the Quarter seemed to be a yearly process. I walked around an awkward man on a ladder boarding up an antique shop. There were also places that seemed built to shut down, with big, solid shutters covering up windows. My coffee shop was already closed, but not yet boarded. Oddly, there were still tourist groups, much smaller than usual, standing on some of the sidewalks: "Here is where Elvis sang from the balcony in *Creole King*." I caught a few phrases each time I walked around one of these groups, patching together my own sense of the stories: "He was living in a furniture store ... blood everywhere ... slaves with broken and strangely reset bones ... today it stands empty." Sometimes these groups would bulge with tourists, forcing me to walk into the street; on this evening, though, they were reduced to an unfortunate few.

Not content with what was left, my mind peopled the streets. Those pathetic mules that pull tourist carriages were already gone, but I could still hear their clomp.

I walked toward the corner that had once been transformed to another era. Film crews had even removed air conditioners to make this corner and its pharmacy look like the forties. A crowd had gathered around, some carrying cameras, all watching for stars. I asked someone staring intently at an empty street, "Who is in this movie?" "Sean Penn and that girl from *Titanic*. What's her name," she answered, pushing the words out with a wet effort. Her tongue was like a hunk of rubber in her mouth. I had to wait and watch with them for a few minutes as artificial rain soaked the intersection, pouring from cranes up high above the buildings. It seemed as though the street might overflow, with no storm in sight. The people—bored, unsure, mesmerized—waited for a glimpse of something to make the day special. (I once saw John Goodman on Bourbon Street.) When Hollywood stopped the rain, I walked through the forties, noticing that some of the old cars seemed to have been intentionally dented in order to look more realistic on film. The crowd that had gathered and waited was still waiting when I left. I read the next day that the stars were nowhere near this set. They had finished filming their scenes more than a week ago and were no longer in New Orleans.

On this day the corner was boarded, abandoned. There were never so many parking spaces on my block.

My apartment was the former slave quarters of a building on Royal, back off from the street, through a bricked-in courtyard. A surprisingly quiet place for the Quarter, even on normal weekends. I lived in the horse stalls, a large room with a couch, stereo, big table for the computer; there was an old brick fireplace, slowly crumbling to dust, in a smaller space that had become my bedroom. Some nights, while trying to fall asleep, I would hear an historic piece of brick fall to the floor. I often wondered who had been in these rooms in the past, but there were no ghosts lingering, or if there were, they did not seem to have any interest in me. My landlady had put in all new appliances, making the place pretty comfortable and causing one friend to say, "I knew those slaves had it easy."

Once, I returned from work and saw a dislocated chameleon on the bluish-green carpet by the television. He seemed too stunned to blend in well, only able to turn into a grey-green. I grabbed a plastic Mardi Gras cup to try and catch him. He jumped to the brown floor, almost matched that brown, and I missed him with my cup. He hopped onto the wall and did very well with the off-white. I was beginning to appreciate his aesthetic efforts. My cup missed again, and he skipped across the carpet into the bathroom. I turned on the light and was insulted. Not funny, little fella. My bathroom floor is not nearly that dirty, sarcastic chameleon. The color he had selected made me want to mop. Instead I scooped him up and carried him to the courtyard. The last I saw of him, he was blending in well with a big tropical green leaf.

Around eleven o'clock I decided to go out and see what the mood of the French Quarter was on this Saturday night. It is difficult to skip a Saturday night when you live right here. There were at least four bars that I liked within two blocks or so of my apartment. Each one was open twenty-four hours. None were for tourists. I hate the past tense. Writing from limbo, after Katrina, there seems to be little choice. The present is in question.

There were still people walking around, not many, but the city was still alive. I turned onto Ursuline and walked on a block that had become much too memorable less than two weeks ago. While walking back to my apartment, around one A.M., I found myself alone on this dark block. (Almost all French Quarter blocks are, or were—at times it feels like the whole story is in this tension between tenses—dark, lit only by gas lights. This lack of light adds to the romance, but does nothing for security.) One A.M. is not especially late here, but it was August, and there were always fewer people around in this humid month. A man rode by on a bicycle. He saw me, circled back and put his bike behind some cars. I kept walking toward home, only around the next corner. He approached. He walked alongside of me, stocky, dark, not young, and put out his hand, asking, "Can you tell me what time it is?" I ignored the offered hand, said, "Nope." Home was only around the corner. "Why won't you shake my hand?" There was a camera up on the corner, on the wall of someone's property. I was walking toward this camera, and about to point it out to him, when I felt a powerful fist connect solidly with the front of my jaw.

He hit me so hard that I could not see. Days later I told a couple of people about this. The word got around, and I found myself telling this story so often that it became fiction. The real details were not for all listeners. This man punched me into my forties, I would tell people. I am thirty-nine now, and this man hit me so hard that I almost turned forty-one. The truth, though, is that this hit stunned me right out of the moment. It did not hurt yet, as I staggered back, toward the wall.

My mind came back to me, although I still could not see, and I realized that this man would try to hurt me some more. He was there, somewhere, and I had to defend myself. Every sense I had focused onto the most primal level—survival. I was forced onto this primal level so firmly, so rudely, that it took me days to recover—to reconnect to civilized life.

The man somehow had me down on the sidewalk and was dragging me toward the street. He wanted more than my wallet. He dragged me over the curb—I saw it drag past—and I felt his firm hand on the back of my neck. Something within me prevented that man from bashing my head against that curb. I got to my hands and knees in the street and yelled for help, a yell that came from a depth far beyond the power of my lungs.

He pulled me over in another direction. I was still stunned, still only able to prevent him, at best, from doing more damage. That was the only thought I could have in this primal blur. He tugged at the back of my pants. What he wanted now I do not know, but I believe only my belt saved me. Another deep yell for help must have resonated through the neighborhood, or perhaps it sounded like some injured animal howling as the car that hit him drove off in the night.

Then he plucked the wallet from my back pocket and was gone.

I got to my knees, in the street, and saw him turning the corner on his bicycle at the other end of the street. I gave one more good yell for help and someone came out on a balcony and asked, "What's going on out there?"

There is nothing macho about this. When the police arrived I was a bleeding, crying, blubbering mess. They took my information. They took down a description. A man in his forties, maybe fifty. A man so prison strong, so Angola strong, that I have no doubt he had spent many angry decades locked away from civilization. Blood dripped to the sidewalk as I talked to the officers. The blood actually seemed to drip through my lip, as if I were drooling blood down my chin. The lower lip was swelling. Four front teeth felt loose. One officer showed me his arm and asked, "Was he about my shade or darker?" "Darker." They took notes, wrote down information, but they did not seem to be in any hurry to find this man who might have been only a few blocks away. It all felt like paperwork.

I finally arrived home around two-thirty and cleaned up the cut on my lip, but I could not test my teeth beneath the swelling. (There were many other scrapes and bruises that I did not notice until the next day.) I needed something sane, so I put on some music (Mingus, Miles), took out a bottle and drank Jack Daniel's until the sun came up.

This too is New Orleans.

On this night, though, New Orleans was trying to decide what to do. I walked past the street corner where Irene's thrived, but the enticement of garlic no longer scented the intersection. Even the best smells had left the city.

I arrived at Harry's bar just past eleven. Harry's was a character-filled place on another corner of the Quarter. It was perfectly situated so that wanderers—locals, visitors or whomever—could come in for a few, adding their stamp to the great catalogue of characters, then wander off to their various lives.

Five nights ago a Tibetan monk walked in. It was past midnight on a Monday night, Tuesday morning, and there were only three of us in the bar—the bartender, Gina, and a local named Gino. Gino, Gina and me. This is not fiction. Two of us had had a few, and in walks an Asian man, wearing a loose-fitting light orange shirt and loose purple pants. Something about the clothes seemed different from those of a typical tourist. Without a word, he caught the attention of the three of us. There was nothing unusual about seeing a lost tourist here, but this man seemed to be more profoundly lost. He took out a scrap of paper and asked, "Where do I go? I have lost everyone." Lost tourists often smile. He did not.

"Well, that depends on what you are looking for," said Gina.

"I am Tibetan monk. You know that? I am lost. Here." He handed the scrap to Gina. The scrap turned out to be of very little help, stray lines to represent streets, scribbles for names. So Gina, seeing no other option, took out the phone book to try and find where a Tibetan monk, lost in New Orleans, should go.

"What do I look up? Monks? Tibet?" She looked at us, then at him. "We don't get too many drunken monks in here."

I spoke to this man. He had been on Bourbon Street, had been drinking a bit, and when he looked around, the other monks were nowhere to be seen. He explained all of this in a level, unexcited tone. Almost uninvolved. Absolutely no panic at being lost in a strange and dangerous city. He was perfectly calm and perfectly lost.

We were unable to get much of a conversation out of him. He just stood there by the bar, patiently waiting, quietly relying on the kindness of these three strangers.

Somehow Gina found a place to send him. Gino said that he had seen prayer flags in that area. Perhaps that scrap had some answers as well. They put the monk in a cab and asked the driver to please bring him back if this turned out to be the wrong destination. The monk said a mild good-bye, and we were left laughing at another oddity of New Orleans.

The air of Harry's was different on this night. There were nine or ten people, but the tone was subdued. Paul the bartender poured my beer and said, "Hey, professor, are you leaving?" I love a place that gets the right drink ready without a word. There were two pint glasses in the bar, kept chilled, and the bartenders who knew me always poured my Abita in one of those glasses. All of the other customers sipped from plastic.

"I think I'm gonna ride it out."

"Me too," and he placed the beer in front of me.

The television was on, and the sound was not drowned out by the music as usual. There was a huge, swirling hurricane in the Gulf.

A man next to me hugged a woman while watching the TV. The woman looked as though she had lost a loved one. He spoke loud enough for the bar to hear, "This is it, man. We're all gonna be up to our fucking necks in water."

The rest of the people tried not to acknowledge this comment. Perhaps he was from somewhere else. People tend not to speak so lightly of their own homes.

I heard a quieter kid next to me saying that he lives on the first floor. "Me too," I told him.

"Are you staying?"

"I'm not sure."

The mayor was on a local channel stating that the levees would not hold for a category-four hurricane. This one was a category five. We could still see it in the corner of the screen as the mayor spoke, growing, swelling with energy, silencing almost everyone in Harry's. The hurricane was expected to hit land on Monday morning.

A weatherman said something after the mayor.

A voice in the bar responded, "Exaggerations, scare tactics. They just want us to keep watching."

Nothing anyone said could prevent that hurricane from looming over the bar. There was almost a science fiction feel to all of this: an ominous force seemed to be approaching, and everyone had to decide whether or not to flee the city. Everyone had to decide what was real.

I must have looked concerned on this Saturday night, because Paul asked, "What are you thinking?"

"I'm thinking this might be the real thing. I'm thinking I might leave."

"Me too. Are you really?"

"I might. What do you think?

"I don't have a car."

"I could give you a ride. Do you want to go?"

"I have cats. Let me think about it."

I heard a woman saying and slurring that she lives in a first floor apartment and that she was—emphatically—"sshtaying."

"This is it. This is the one," repeated the greasy man next to me, making his woman hug him harder.

They were now showing a live shot of the traffic out of

town. It was moving surprisingly well, they said.

I pushed my empty glass forward.

"Another?"

"Yep." He refilled it. "I don't know, Paul. This might be the time to go."

"I can't leave until morning. I have to board this place up."

"It's your life," chirped the kid. "You could tell us all to leave right now. We would understand."

"I'm not the owner, though," Paul said and walked off, talking on his cellphone.

I sipped and began to think that I should go right now. The traffic was not bad; it would be much worse in the morning. I could see it on TV, bumper to bumper but moving.

The beer was good after the hot day, but Harry's was starting to feel stagnant.

"Paul, I'm thinking about going right now. Tomorrow is going to suck."

"I have a ride."

"Are you sure? 'Cause I will wait."

"No, I'm set. Are you going?"

"I'm going now," I said and finished down the beer.

"You are really going now?" the kid asked.

"Yep, my car is two blocks from here."

"Chug that beer."

"Alright, professor," Paul said, looking concerned, looking like he did not want to be behind the bar. Katrina raged on the radar. "Take care of yourself."

As I left Harry's, no one seemed to be moving. Everyone was staring at that hurricane, trying to decide.

The street was next to desolate as I walked to the corner store. At the Verti Marte I bought a couple of gallons of water. Back at my apartment I stuffed a few days of clothes into a bag. I unplugged the television, computer, putting the plugs up as high as possible. I placed a rug on top of a bookshelf.

I put some food in another bag and walked out to my car.

It was midnight. The Quarter was still and quiet, almost peaceful, as I left it.

The streets felt empty as I drove to the freeway. In six years of living here I have learned how emptiness, death, in New Orleans, often lends itself to a celebration, perhaps a parade. This is not a style. It is a philosophy, a foundation for a culture. On this night that sense of triumph was missing, and when it comes again, this city should elevate it, place it on a stage. The first trumpet to return wins.

Onto the freeway by the Superdome, up the ramp, and the traffic was not bad yet. After ten minutes I caught up to it. As I slowed almost to a stop, I saw the red brake lights of cars heading far into the distance, as far as I could see.

The cars moved, not quickly, but they moved, for hours and hours, as I drove through the night, toward Houston. It felt like a three-hundred-mile funeral procession.

Voices I.

RAY NAGIN, AARON NEVILLE,
STEVEN ROHBOCK, STRANGEBONE

```
----Original Message----
From: Green, Matthew
Sent: Monday, August 29, 2005 9:50 AM
To: Buikema, Edward
Cc: Lowder, Michael
Subject: Re: Information

From WWL TV


... A LEVEE BREACH OCCURRED ALONG THE INDUSTRIAL CANAL AT
TENNESSE [sic] STREET. 3 TO 8 FEET OF WATER IS EXPECTED DUE
TO THE BREACH ... LOCATIONS IN THE WARNING INCLUDE BUT ARE
NOT LIMITED TO ARABI AND 9TH WARD OF NEW ORLEANS.


Matthew Green
FEMA Hurricane Liaison Team Coordinator
National Hurricane Center
1169 SW 17th Street
Miami, Florida 33165-2149 USA
```

----Original Message----
From: Heath, Michael
Sent: Monday, August 29, 2005 10:12 AM
To: Rhode, Patrick; Altshuler, Brooks; Burris, Ken
Subject: Re: Superdome

From Marty Bahamonde in the New Orleans EOC (next to the superdome)

-Severe flooding on the St. Bernard/Orleans parish line. Police report water level up to second floor of two story houses. People are trapped in attics.

- Pumps starting to fail. The city has now confirmed four pumps are off line.

- Windows and parts of the east side of the Amaco [sic] building blown out.
- New Orleans shopping center (next to superdome) destroyed.
- Windows and parts of the east side of the Hyatt Hotel have been blown out. Furniture is blowing out of the hotel.
- Top floors of the Entergy building have been blown out.
- Area around the Superdome is beginning to flood.

We should have pictures shortly.

RAY NAGIN

Ray Nagin was born in New Orleans in 1956. He graduated from Tuskegee in 1978 with a degree in accounting. He earned an MBA from Tulane in 1994. Nagin was vice president at the cable company Cox Communications before running for mayor of the city. He had no political experience at the time. He was elected mayor of New Orleans in 2002, three months after changing his party affiliation from Republican to Democrat. The following is from an interview with Garland Robinette of the radio station WWL on September 1, 2005.

You call him [the president] right now, and you call the governor, and you tell them to delegate the power that they have to the mayor of New Orleans and we'll get this damn thing fixed. It's politics, man, and they playing games and they spinning. They out there spinning for the cameras ...

I've talked directly with the president. I've talked to the head of the Homeland Security. I've talked to everybody under the sun. I've been out there, man. I flew these helicopters, been in the crowds, talking to people crying, don't know where their relatives are. I've done it all, man, and I tell you, man, Garland, I keep hearing that it's coming. This is coming, that is coming. And my answer to that today is B.S. Where is the beef? Because there is no beef in this city. There is no beef anywhere in Southeast Louisiana. And these goddamn ships that are coming, I don't see 'em ...

I basically told him we had an incredible, uh, crisis here and that his flying over in Air Force One does not do it justice. And that I have been all around this city, and I am very frustrated because we are not able to marshal resources and we're outmanned in just about every respect. You know the reason why the looters got out of control? Because we had most of our resources saving people, thousands of people that were stuck in attics, man, old ladies. When you pull off the doggone ventilator vent and you look down there and they're standing in there in water up to their fricking necks.

And they don't have a clue what's going on down here. They flew down here one time two days after the doggone event was over with TV cameras, AP reporters, all kind of goddamn, excuse my French everybody in America, but I am pissed …

And I am telling you right now, they're showing all these reports of people looting and doing all that weird stuff, and they are doing that, but people are desperate, and they're trying to find food and water, the majority of them. Now you got some knuckleheads out there, and they are taking advantage of this lawless—this situation where, you know, we can't really control it, and they're doing some awful, awful things. But that's a small majority [sic] of the people. Most people are looking to try and survive.

And you've got—and one of the things people—nobody's talking about this. Drugs flowed in and out of New Orleans and the surrounding metropolitan area so freely it was scary to me, and that's why we were having the escalation in murders. People don't want to talk about this, but I'm a talk about it. You have drug addicts that are now walking around this city looking for a fix, and that's the reason why they were breaking in hospitals and drugstores. They're looking for something to take the edge off of their jones, if you will.

And right now, they don't have anything to take the edge off. And they've probably found guns. So what you're seeing is drug-starving crazy addicts, drug addicts, that are wreakin' havoc. And we don't have the manpower to adequately deal with it. We can only target certain sections of the city and form a perimeter around 'em and hope to God that we're not overrun …

*

And I'll, I'll tell you man, I, I am, I'm probably going to get in a whole bunch of trouble. I'm probably going to get in so much trouble it ain't even funny …

But we authorized eight billion dollars to go to Iraq lickety-sp—quick. After 9/11 we gave the president unprecedented powers lickety-s—quick to take care of New York and other places. Now, you mean to tell me that a place where most of your oil is coming through, a place that is so unique when you mention New Orleans anywhere around the world everybody's eyes light up, you mean to tell me that a place where you probably have thousands of people that have died and thousands more that are dying every day, that we can't figure out a way to authorize the resources that we need? Come on, man.

You know, I'm not one of those drug addicts. I am thinking very clearly. And I don't know whose problem it is. I don't know whether it's the governor's problem. I don't know whether it's the president's problem, but somebody need to get their ass on a plane and sit down, the two of them, and figure this out, right now …

I don't want to see anybody do anymore goddamn press conferences. Put a moratorium on press conferences. Don't do another press conference until the resources are in this city. And then come down to this city and stand with us when there are military trucks and troops that we can't even count. Don't tell me forty-thousand people are coming here. They're not here. It's too doggone late. Now get off your asses and let's do something, and let's fix the biggest goddamn crisis in the history of this country …

People are dying. They don't have homes. They don't have jobs. [*pause*] The city of New Orleans will never be the same [*pause*] in this time. [*pause, a muffled sound of sniffling, breathing*] I got to go.

AARON NEVILLE

Singer Aaron Neville had lived his whole life in New Orleans until Katrina. Born in 1941, the third of four brothers, he was raised in the city's Calliope housing projects. Inspired by the singing of his older brother Art, Aaron recorded for several local labels until he broke out with the number-one hit "Tell It Like It Is" in 1966. Eleven years after that, he and his siblings formed the Neville Brothers and recorded a string of successful albums. Each year the brothers conclude the New Orleans Jazz Fest, finishing their set with "Amazing Grace." Following are excerpts from his interview with Rolling Stone *magazine, published on September 22, 2005.*

Everybody from down there, you can hear the New Orleans beat in their music. From the Marsalis family, to Harry Connick Jr., to Dr. John, the Nevilles—it's in them. There was a rhythm to the city. When Mardi Gras came, I got a chance to get a little further away from the projects. We'd see the Indian bands, and that fascinated all of us. It was a melting pot of different cultures, music and food. We had the French, the Spanish, the Irish, the Italian. The Nevilles have some Native American in us. I call myself Heinz 57. It was a cultural gumbo down there, and right now it's a toxic gumbo.

It will be a while before I go back. Right now I'll leave it as a memory, and remember it as the city that I grew up in. The way it looks now, with all the toxic stuff down there, I don't know if I'll be able to return to New Orleans in my lifetime. And it's not going to be the same. I hear people talking about making New Orleans better. That would be good. I hope they can.

————Original Message————
From: Worthy, Sharon
Sent: Sunday, September 4, 2005 10:17 AM
To: michael d. brown
Subject: Your shirt

Please roll up the sleeves of your shirt ... all shirts. Even the President rolled his sleeves to just above the elbow.

In this crisis and on TV you just need to look more hard-working ... ROLL UP THE SLEEVES!

STEVEN ROHBOCK
Steven Rohbock is a jazz pianist and a New Orleans native. He evacuated to Chicago after Katrina and began looking for work to support his family.

I got a connection through one of the local churches. They gave us a number of things, clothing, a list of different restaurants that hire musicians. I found a Greek restaurant that was in the process of hiring a new pianist. I called the union—I'm in the union down in New Orleans—to register and they gave me a free card with honorary membership until the end of the year. I think they felt that this guy's from New Orleans, so let's cut him a break.

I play at the Greek restaurant Friday, Saturday and Sunday. It's definitely helping out. People who have met me or have read about me in the newspaper or seen me on TV come by and throw in tip money. I don't know how long that is going to last.

We lost everything. Our house was on 17th Street and Canal. It has nine feet of water. We heard stories from people and we thought maybe it would be in two feet of

SWAMP SCENE NEAR NEW ORLEANS

water, but no … probably nothing is usable because of the mold, the thick stuff caked on the walls.

We put stuff on the second floor in the bedroom—all our clothing—but it's probably unusable. We left Sunday morning around four A.M. I had a late afternoon gig on Bourbon Street and then I was supposed to play contemporary jazz at a cigar bar in Uptown, but when I got there at ten-thirty at night, it was all boarded up.

Storms come through New Orleans every year. Usually, the hurricanes end up going somewhere else. I got home early and started putting stuff upstairs. We put stuff on the kitchen table because we thought we might get a couple of feet of water.

Around four or five, we got our vehicles. We have a large van that my wife just bought for her company. We took the other car and left it at the airport parking lot on the sixth floor. But we heard that the police were stealing cars. Our gas tank was almost full, so I'm sure they took it. And we only had two months of car payments left.

Next week, we're going to go back and see if we can find it. Sometimes we have glimmers of hope, but I'm pretty sure everything we owned is destroyed.

My son is five. His name is Shouki. He understands what is going on. He knows his house is under water. He was pretty mad that we didn't pack more of his toys. And we could have. We have this big van.

Whether it was the Corps of Engineers or the funds being cut by Bush … In any case, it broke. Panels went flying. The levee was like our backyard. We used to play on the levee, take cork board and slide down the dirt mounds. The eight-foot wall gave way and collapsed a little farther down from our house—about half a mile.

I don't know if there is anything there to salvage but we have to go back and look. We won't get the one-thousand-dollar security deposit from the landlady. I wish we would, but we won't. We may go in and start cleaning the place up or we may just walk in, look at it and leave. I'm hoping we find our car. I'm not expecting it. The cops probably took it. They know how to break in and hotwire cars. They're experts.

We kept trying to apply for aid from FEMA over the Internet. We would get through the first two pages, and it would freeze up cause we were on dial-up. Finally, we got to the last page and sent it out. It turns out we were applying multiple times so they said we're not eligible for any relief. Can you believe that shit? We lost everything.

When I called FEMA, most people were rude. They would get real pissy. "You just have to wait!" Everybody I know got something and we got nothing. And we lost everything! Friends had hotels paid for, they got two-thousand dollars ... Finally, they told us to wait forty-eight hours. Four days go by and there's nothing. So I call and they say, "There's no forty-eight hours. You just got to wait." Jerks!

The local churches were the only places that have worked for us. They gave us a piano, washing machines. People in this area have been really kind, almost to the point of discomfort.

I have to direct my anger at something. With FEMA, I'm furious. But I can't get angry at Mother Nature. It just happened and we weren't prepared.

STRANGEBONE

A man who called himself Strangebone talked with New York Times *reporter Dan Barry in early September 2005 on Clouet Street. He told Barry that the police had beaten him and taken his gun, and then he added the following comment about the post-Katrina sky.*

You're able to see the stars. It's wonderful.

*

We're Getting Out of Here.

BILL LAVENDER *talks to* JOHN GRAVOIS

WHEN WE HEARD ABOUT THE STORM, we decided not to evacuate, because we really didn't think our house was in grave danger. We live in Mid-City, which is a part of New Orleans that's
relatively high but not as high as the French Quarter. It's an old
house. It's been through plenty of hurricanes.

I guess the storm was at full force at midmorning on Monday. It never was really that bad—I actually put on my motor-
cycle helmet and walked around outside at the height of it. We
lost power, of course. We still had water, we still had gas.

By about two o'clock in the afternoon, the storm was over.
There was a little bit of water in the street, but nothing I couldn't
have driven through. Our reaction at that point was, Well, this
wasn't really that bad.

If that had been all the storm was, I wouldn't have regret-
ted staying.

At some point in there, the water did start to rise. It was rising
in the full sunshine, with no rain, just coming up in the streets.

Our neighbor across the street, who had evacuated, had
a boat under her house — a fourteen-foot light aluminum skiff
with oarlocks and oars. As kind of a lark, I went and pulled it
out from under her house and put it in the street.

That night, Monday night, we went out on the front porch. There was absolutely no light, and there was no noise, and the stars were fantastically clear.

We got up the next morning, and the water was higher. We were trying to listen to the radio, trying to figure out what was going on. We were hearing that the flooding on the east side of New Orleans was really bad. We were starting to hear helicopters flying around.

There was a rumor that the levee was broken somewhere, but that they were going to be fixing it, and that as soon as they got the levee fixed, they were going to be able to pump the water out. I was thinking maybe the end of the week at the most.

One of my neighbors came to my door and said there was a guy around the corner with a baby who needed to go to the hospital. The guy was scared to death of water.

So we got in the boat, and we were rowing down the street, trying to pick the best route to Mercy Hospital. There was water all the way — right up to the front door.

Some guy in scrubs got down in the water and helped me dock the boat there on the steps. He was a paramedic who worked for the city. He said they had no power in the hospital, and he had a generator down at his office. He wanted to know if I could row him down there so he could get this generator.

And I asked him, "Doesn't the hospital have backup power?" He said, "Yeah, they have a generator, but it's in the basement."

It was ludicrous, this notion of going to get a five-thousand-watt generator to power a hospital. But he said, "There are people dying in here, and it's all we can do."

So we went to his paramedic station, a little two-story metal building. Two of his colleagues were there.

This guy I'm with told them, "I've come to get the generator." And they told him no. He said, "Look, there are people dying in Mercy."

"Well things are tough all over, and before this generator comes out of here, I've got to get me and my dogs out."

43.

At that point, I kind of exploded. I said, "You're not even using the generator. The generator has nothing to do with your dogs." It kind of shamed them. We finally did get the generator.

We had our last good meal that night. We were having wine on the front porch, all the neighbors were out on their porches, and I got out my guitar and sang "A Hard Rain's A-Gonna Fall."

That night it was really hot and really still. There were helicopters messing around all night. I had this idea they were either evacuating Mercy Hospital or bringing them a generator. At one point they were so close that I could feel the wind, so I took to praying for them to come over.

It wasn't until Wednesday that we started to get more information. There was a press conference at twelve. They said they thought the levee repairs would be done by about Friday. Then they said they should have the water out of the city within about thirty days. I said, "We're getting out of here. We can't live like this for thirty days."

We packed up very hastily — all our drinking water and a good bit of food. I left my hard drive with thirty years of miscellaneous writings on it, plus Nancy's hard drive with all her scholarship on it. I just tried to hide them in the attic. I didn't know what else to do.

We had to put our cat in a carrying cage, and we put our dogs on the boat. We went and got our neighbor, my friend Charlie Franklin. We told him what we'd heard and we told him it's time to go. He thought about it for about two minutes and then said OK.

We were nervous. We knew there were no police. We'd been warned that there were roving bands of armed looters. We knew that the boat was becoming a valuable commodity. The dogs were nervous also. They would not let anyone approach closer than about ten feet from the boat. Charlie had a gun.

When we turned one corner, there was a kiddie pool floating in the middle of Canal Street, and I could see a head sticking up over the side of it. There was another guy pushing it and another guy wandering around in the chest-deep water looking kind of dreamy. They were junkies that had looted the Rite Aid. They were using this kiddie pool to get out of the water to shoot up.

A little further, there was a dead man in the water. Someone had hung his shirt up on a street sign. I couldn't really see his face, but the shirt was sticking up like a tent. We heard later they were tying corpses to street signs and poles.

Across the street was a building called the City Hall Annex. It has a big front porch that was just above water level, and it was full of people, maybe 150. On one end, there were women and kids holding up signs saying, "Help us please." At the other end of the porch there was this mad party going on. They were breaking windows and throwing whiskey bottles around and kind of whooping and yelling.

We were starting to get very careful about our route because we were getting close to the Superdome, and we didn't want to get caught there. Our plan was to go to the Macy's parking lot, which is just adjacent to the dome, where we had parked our car. We were just praying that we might be able to get to the car and drive out.

There were no cops. In this whole ride, we never saw a cop.

When we got to the Macy's parking lot, we saw that the entrance was four feet deep. So we couldn't get our car. We followed the water to the corner of Girod and Carondolet, and that's where the water ended. We had to abandon the boat.

So we started walking uptown to go to my ex-wife's house, which we knew was dry, and they had a generator and probably food and water. For all I knew, they were still there, because I hadn't talked to them since Monday morning when the phones went out.

We saw this two-story house with the facade completely removed. It was just like a dollhouse. I could see the furniture and the bookshelves, everything neat, nothing in disarray, and these two black labs up on the second floor looking down at us.

After a while, a guy caught up with us. He told us he had walked all the way from the Lower Ninth Ward. I'm guessing that must be at least five miles. He told us that down in the Ninth Ward he was literally wading through bodies on the way out. He didn't know where any of his family was. He had a three-year-old and a five-year-old kid, and he suspected that they were both dead. He was coming uptown because he had a brother who was a butler in a Garden District mansion.

He told us that in the end there will be tens of thousands dead.

We got to my ex's house. We were just praying that we were going to see her pickup outside the house. But there was nothing, and our hearts just sank. We'd been on the road now for about four to five hours. We were exhausted.

Then I remembered that our friends lived just a few blocks away, and they had left their car. Not only that, but I knew right where the key was. We got to Alex and Kat's house, and the car was intact, and the key was in the mailbox. But we couldn't make the key work in the door. I tried it and Charlie tried it, and finally I said, "Charlie, move," and I threw a brick through the window.

We crammed all of us in the car. We drove to Tchoupitoulas Street and then straight across the bridge to the West Bank, the only way out.

The next day, we were going to leave Charlie in Baton Rouge to take the bus to Alexandria, but we found out that there were 200,000 people downtown trying to get out. So we took him all the way to Alexandria. We started to have the emotional breakdown. It was strange how, going through the whole thing, I just sort of never stopped. None of us did.

But when we dropped Charlie off, all three of us broke down and started crying and pretty much didn't stop for about three days.

The Holy City of New Orleans.

JASON BERRY

HEMINGWAY CALLED COURAGE "grace under pressure." I saw that grace in great display after Hurricane Katrina bore down, grace entwined with another kind of valor: the realization that in order to be brave, you must first be afraid.

My wife, Melanie McKay, and I left our house in the Carrollton neighborhood of New Orleans to ride out the storm with my brother, Lamar, and his family in Covington, a leafy town across Lake Pontchartrain, fifty miles north of the city.

My mother, Mary Frances, eighty-four, was with us. She lived at Chateau Notre Dame, an assisted-living facility under the auspices of the New Orleans archdiocese, which evacuated residents without kin to care for them to Baton Rouge. The Chateau dwarfs the archdiocesan chancery building and lies a block from my home. Mother visited several times a week to spend time with Ariel, my fourteen-year-old daughter, a Down syndrome child no longer in school because of health reasons. Ariel's mother and I parted many years ago but we have co-parented well, sharing custody in houses less than ten minutes' drive from each other.

Six of us would ride out the storm in Covington—Mary Frances; Lamar and Ellen and their twenty-one-year-old son

Zachary; Melanie and I. We married in December 2004 after the slow waltz of a midlife courtship. Our house in New Orleans, recently renovated, was filled with books and paintings. We traveled light, assuming we'd return in a few days or a week at most.

My daughters, Simonette, twenty, and Ariel, left with their mother in a three-car caravan (including pets) by another route, along Highway 90, straddling the Mississippi River until the road veers west to Cajun country, where my former wife and her siblings grew up, and their mother lives today.

Evacuations are a ritual of recent vintage. People rarely left in the 1950s, when I was growing up, nor in the 1960s, a decade of two horrific hurricanes—Betsy, in 1965, which flooded the Lower Ninth Ward, and Camille, which shattered the Mississippi Gulf Coast in 1969. Seventeen people died in one apartment building in Camille. They refused to leave despite warnings by the janitor; they were ripping out corks for a party. In parishes across New Orleans, a prayer was regularly intoned in the August-to-October hurricane season: "Our Lady of Prompt Succor, pray for us … spare us from the storm."

The ferocity of hurricanes intensified in the 1990s. Whether global warming produced this I cannot say, but they have become a greater and more consistent threat. Hurricane Georges in 1998 caused city officials to warn people to leave if they could. That was a coded message to those with the means to depart. The highways were jammed with outbound cars. Yet one knew that many people would stay behind. For however rich we were in culture, cuisine and the rocking good times of a city that gave jazz music to the world, the poor were always close at hand. The city was sixty-three percent African-American, of whom half lived at or below the poverty level. When the exodus began for Katrina, thousands had no way to leave.

In Covington, the lights went out sometime before dawn. Katrina's fury was terrifying. The sky swirled gray as wind sheets uprooted massive oaks and pines, lashing the earth like a giant with a bullwhip, searing lawns, pummeling roads, cutting gashes and grooves, scattering trees like shards of leather. The wind blasted out the bay window in the living room with the high, keening wail of some creature out of hell. Then came an eerie whooshing sound, intercut by bursts and cracks as tree torsos kept popping. The wind shifted to a deep bellow as I watched the Bogue Falaya River surge, though not as high as the house.

With power gone, we listened on battery-operated radio to WWL Radio 870 AM, the fifty-thousand-watt Clear Channel station that has done live coverage of hurricanes since my childhood. I am a native son of New Orleans. I had a good life there as a writer and documentary producer. As the house in Covington grew steamy, we heard WWL News Director Dave Cohen interview city Councilman Oliver Thomas, who had been out on a boat rescuing folk from the flooded downriver wards. Thomas pleaded to people in adjacent Jefferson Parish, a white flight suburb: "We got to be tolerant, people. We got to pull together; we are all one area now."

Jefferson Parish President Aaron Broussard made regular trips to WWL, warning people to leave amid a surreal play-by-play of what he was seeing in Kenner. He spoke of an apartment building on Manhattan Boulevard. "The miracle on Manhattan it was once called. Well it'll be a miracle if anybody in there comes out alive." He came back later to say it was gone. At some point, Lake Pontchartrain began to pour into the city and the surrounding suburbs. Mayor C. Ray Nagin, a tough and candid presence, showed strong leadership in those initial days. The politicians embodied grace under pressure.

President Bush showed cowardice and incompetence. A commander in chief's first job is to protect the citizenry. Bush failed shamefully, flying over the city on his way back from another vacation on his ranch in Texas. LBJ was in New Orleans on the heels of Hurricane Betsy, inspecting damage and talking to people. As the enormity of loss and suffering set in, news director Cohen was a haggard voice: "Where do I live? New Orleans is over." Yet he and others at the station soldiered on. So did *The Times-Picayune*, which reassembled in Baton Rouge to put out a Web edition, posting its prophetic 2002 series on the fragile levee system and chronicling life after Katrina.

Almost overnight, New Orleans became a legacy of the naked cynicism of George W. Bush's environmental policies and the spurning of many requests for levee restoration. Ray Nagin lost his cool at the end of the week, cursing the failure of federal authorities to evacuate the Superdome and Convention Center and send troops to fight the marauding criminals. But Nagin gave voice to the anguish of those stranded at the Convention Center and Superdome, which was built a half mile from the site of Louis Armstrong's birth. Louis grew up dancing behind the brass bands in street parades, known as second lines. The second liners with their spontaneous choreographies charged the city's folkways with a sense of myth and connection to the African mother culture. Many of those poor folk ended up stranded in the dark, cavernous buildings as the world watched aghast.

One of the lucky ones who got out was Fats Domino, the seventy-seven-year-old rhythm-and-blues icon who lived in a baronial mansion in the Lower Ninth Ward, surrounded by sagging shotgun houses and ramshackle homes with clapboards peeling. With all of his wealth from millions of recording sales, the Fat Man (as he is lovingly called) didn't, or wouldn't, leave. He was evacuated by boat with several family members to the Superdome and from there by bus to an evacuation center in Baton Rouge. They went to stay in the apartment of JaMarcus Russell, the quarterback of the LSU Tigers football team; his girlfriend's family was friendly with the Dominos.

Countless stories of strangers helping strangers permeate these ravaged latitudes—people taking in strangers, giving money, food, rides, cellphones—the grace of hands across the table, reaching to those in need. By the end of the week my eighty-two-year-old uncle Lanier Devine, having evacuated by car to Colleyville, Texas, near Fort Worth, was in a hospital battling pneumonia. I managed to get there three weeks later, a few hours before he died. We held his funeral with Texas cousins at hand. One of my first cousins landed in Houston and managed to place her son in a good school to continue eighth grade. My stepson and his family relocated to Houston after their home in Lakeview took eight feet of water—everything lost. The contours of Katrina's diaspora and the legacy of those losses will mark many of us forever.

For four days fallen trees kept us trapped in Covington, where Walker Percy set his famous comic novel, *Love in the Ruins: The Adventures of a Bad Catholic at a Time Near the End of the World.* I joined an upscale chain gang, a group of guys buzzing through trees with chain saws bought via a supply line of people marching through suburban yards to catch rides with well-heeled neighbors to Home Depot, which sold the chain saws that kept conking out. The lead cutter was a French yoga instructor named Bruno; he wielded that chain saw like a fencer with a foil. Percy, a supreme ironist who lived on the other side of the Bogue Falaya, would have appreciated Bruno were he still alive. Scrubbing my scalp with shampoo in a hot tub filled with pine needles and not much heat, I thought of Walker often. He got me my first book contract. He was rare, as writers go, for being such a virtuous man, deeply religious, with a marvelous eye on the human experiment. His novels registered a belief that disasters draw people together, giving life more rarified meaning from the ennui of daily living. By week's end, I had red splotches of poison ivy on hands, chest and legs from the wood cutting and log lifting, and one itchy splotch where the sun don't shine. The following week, in St. Martinville, a physician gave me a shot and put me on steroids, which eventually eliminated the rash but produced insomnia and perhaps augmented my rage at Little George Bush.

We passed dank, steamy nights in the big house, eating canned food, trying to sleep in the heat, wondering about friends whose whereabouts we knew not and grieving for the city with a

VIEW IN REAR
OF
ST LOUIS CATHEDREL

E. M. LAW

FROM PHOTO LILIENTHAL

sorrow embedded like a sword in the heart. My brother bought a portable generator to restart his appliances; the land line kept working after the cellphones lost juice, until the fourth and final day of the tree cutting. Somehow Bell South fell victim to the road clearing.

We left on Friday. Melanie and I drove Mary Frances to Baton Rouge, hoping to reunite her with the Chateau residents. We found them at St. George's, a Catholic high school, where the gym had become a huge dormitory. Two women on the staff had traveled with the elderly evacuees, some in wheelchairs and on portable oxygen. Linda Brumfield and Alice Stockard were angels of virtue. We said goodbye to them with embraces and tears, and drove on to New Iberia, settling mother in a welcoming facility, recently built. Later that night, I learned that Linda and Alice had no jobs. There was no place to work; they received cash severances. Linda, a trained medical worker, was in a Red Cross shelter in Hammond, trying to find a place to live in Baton Rouge. Alice went back to Kenner. I established phone contact with Linda and have been in touch intermittently—the spotty cellphone service is maddening—and sent five-hundred dollars to help her find a place to live. Alice I still hope to find.

I will miss the life we had, terribly so. Every week an elderly black man cut my grass with his son and another guy. I paid him thirty dollars and called him Mr. Joyner. He called me Jason. Many a time he said: "How's yo' momma? Tell yo' momma I said hi. Tell her I miss cuttin' her grass." Where are you, Mr. Joyner?

I loved the way black women called men my age "baby" and the lazy rhythms of the calliope blowing off the river; I treasured the second line parades and the funerals and the bonds I had with so many musicians about whom I wrote for years. I wonder if I will hear another sermon by Fr. Dave Boileau, a towering septuagenarian (and ex-chaplain for the Teamsters), at Mater Dolorosa Church on Carrollton Avenue. He kept his homilies focused on our responsibilities to "the other" and threw in quotes by Dostoevski to boot. Dave, I hope you are well and somewhere dry.

I loved the ritual of drinking wine—and on special days old-fashioneds—once or twice a week with my best friend since kindergarten, Kenny Charbonnet, in the solarium of my home. Two sons of the South, one a Democrat, the other a Republican, relished the society of our small place in the sun, while just outside the window lizards danced on the riot of green philodendron and elephant ears and palmetto leaves. God, I loved that city and the beauty of what we had.

The crime and poverty were always there. My garage was invaded three times so I quit locking it.

You could not live in the city and avoid the dreary performance of democracy; yet the town was held together by a spiritual essence few cities in this country possess. We were like many families in having those we loved most within a short drive. That infrastructure of the heart is severely fractured now.

With so many people living in other people's spare bedrooms, real estate began booming in the region from Baton Rouge west to Cajun country, which is starting to resemble a mining camp. Like Blanche DuBois, the addled character in Tennessee Williams' play *A Streetcar Named Desire*, we in the broken lower Gulf South must rely "on the kindness of strangers." I hope the grace shown by so many here strikes the consciences of the social Darwinists who rule Congress. This region cannot rebuild without a massive infusion of money, which means raising taxes, lest we fight a second war on a credit card, as Bush is doing in Iraq.

My wife and I spent three weeks in Lafayette, where a population of 120,000 strains to absorb forty-thousand souls from the diaspora. In the home where we stayed, another couple learned that their house in Metairie burned down. Our neighborhood took three feet of water, but on a brief trip into the city, I found the house largely undamaged. The city smelled like the world's oldest outhouse. How does one go back to a case study in epidemiology research?

And yet at moments like this, one cherishes life as a gift. My little girl will see both her grandmothers regularly. Simonette went off to Boston University for the fall semester, the Tulane scholarship transferred for credit. As I write, in late October, countless streets are lined with dead refrigerators and piles of debris with shards of drywall stacked up like cardboard. Melanie is in Houston helping with her grandchildren. I write these lines in a guest room in the home of my friend Adam Nossiter, a correspondent for the *Times*. Each afternoon I go back to my house, wearing a mouth mask to clear out soggy stuff from the garage. I am told the electricity will be on in the house in another week, or two. The city has fired three-thousand workers and is dead broke. The epidemiological issues are gigantic. Yet each day one sees a new stirring of life, another restaurant opened, lights on in another house. How many people will return? What kind of city will it be? In this strange, rootless configuration of our lives, the pull of family is a constant, and for now and perhaps forever I will think of you, my dear sweet flooded place, as what you were and are in my heart—the holy city of New Orleans.

*

Voices II.

BARBARA BUSH, WYNTON MARSALIS,
DENNIS KUCINICH, STEVE QUINN

BARBARA BUSH

The former first lady of the United States was interviewed on September 5, 2005, during a tour of the Reliant Center in Houston, an eight-thousand-seat arena that was home to eleven-thousand evacuees from New Orleans. The interview was conducted for American Public Media's "Marketplace."

I'm bursting with pride, so much so that almost everyone I talk to says that we're gonna move to Houston …

We had a mother who had two little, who had twins, that were, I think, a month old, almost, who stood on a bridge for three days with no food, and she's grateful to be here. Little twin boys. But, it, it [*baby cries in the background*], Houston is a miracle to these people …

What I'm hearing, which is sort of scary, is they all want to stay in Texas … and so many of the people in the arenas here are, uh, you know, were, uh, were underprivileged anyway, so this is working very well [*chuckles*] for them.

WYNTON MARSALIS

The trumpet great spoke before the National Press Club on October 20, 2005. His talk was entitled "Higher Ground: Hurricane Relief and Rebuilding New Orleans." In the question and answer period after the talk, he was asked to respond to Barbara Bush's comment.

I don't like to talk about anybody's mama. [*laughter*] I'm a just put that out there for y'all. [*laughter and applause*] And though George Bush is the president, and people like to speak, I think, and Clinton's, very disrespectfully, I have respect for the office of the president, and I'm not gonna talk about the man's mama. I don't agree with what she said. That's all I'm gonna say.

DENNIS KUCINICH

Kucinich is a congressman from Ohio. The following remarks are from the Congressional Record of September 8, 2005.

Mr. Speaker, for the people of the Gulf Coast region who were stricken by Hurricane Katrina, there is less to the emergency supplemental than meets the eye. I mean that exactly zero dollars of the fifty-billion dollars Congress will send today for emergency relief and temporary construction will be used for employing people displaced by Hurricane Katrina. However, the administration is not withholding anything from Halliburton. Halliburton received a no-bid contract immediately after the hurricane. Yet the CBO estimates 400,000 people were made unemployed by the hurricane.

For the region, the economic devastation is on par with the effects of the Great Depression. At that time, President Roosevelt asked for a National Industrial Recovery Act with which the government put millions of people back to work rebuilding the country's infrastructure. That is what the hurricane-demolished region needs today. The people of the region who have lost their livelihoods should be given preference in hiring for the federal dollars spent, and the federal dollars should be conditioned on local hiring targets.

But this is not a New Deal administration. Instead of leveraging federal tax money to put people back to work, the administration is content to send Halliburton billions of dollars in no-bid contracts.

STEVE QUINN

Steve Quinn is an energy reporter in the Dallas bureau of Associated Press. He was dispatched to the Gulf Coast region soon after Katrina struck to survey the damage from Pascagoula, Mississippi, to New Orleans.

I had no intention of leaving the trailer until it was time to drive out of the city, for I had seen enough of the carnage Hurricane Katrina wrought on New Orleans—even just for a day. But an Associated Press colleague, whom I had met that morning, minced no words when she said: "Go to the end of the street and get your shots."

Mary Foster, a New Orleans-based writer, implored more than she did suggest that it would be a good idea to get immunized for tetanus, hepatitis B and hepatitis A. "I'm serious. If you haven't had your shots, don't take any chances. It won't take long and it's just at the end of the street."

And so I left one of three AP trailers sitting in front of a Sheraton hotel in the middle of Canal Street, home to a stretch of vehicles owned or rented by national media outlets.

Were it not for category-four Hurricane Katrina, Canal would be teeming with cars, cabs and limousines serving the central business district and its famed nightlife in the adjacent French Quarter. Its sidewalks would be packed with business travelers headed toward Harrah's New Orleans Casino, or in search of some Cajun food, or maybe a taste of the city's blues or jazz scene. Instead, Canal featured media crowds grossly outnumbered by the sum of military and law enforcement personnel maintaining order in a city suddenly silenced by Katrina.

Five minutes after leaving the trailer and just before reaching the medical station at the end of Canal, I looked to my left and saw a Wyndham hotel. Then I took a closer look at the area. I stopped and said aloud, "Holy shit. I've been here before. But it wasn't anything like this. Not at all."

No one heard me. It wasn't meant for anyone to hear, and if anyone had, I wouldn't have cared. I was too stunned. The change this city had undergone struck a different nerve.

I could suddenly engage other senses to detect stark change. I could still smell the dank presence of the flooding long after the waters receded, even as I came in over the Crescent City Expressway. What I should have been looking forward to was indigenous scents from bakeries, restaurants and spilled drinks on the sidewalk. It had been eight years since I had last passed through New Orleans. Then, I got hungry every five minutes walking by restaurants serving up catfish or red beans and rice or the pungent yet refreshing odor from steamed crawfish and shrimp.

I could hear more air traffic than I would if I were standing near a busy municipal airport. But today, the sounds came from the military choppers flying overhead, close enough to drown out some conversation. My time spent in three Mississippi cities—Biloxi, Gulfport and Pascagoula—acclimated my senses to know that these aircraft were the norm. I no longer instinctively looked up. The noise was as commonplace as a child crying in a maternity ward.

My daylong journey in New Orleans didn't take me to the worst areas, but it didn't keep me from seeing enough to know that something was terribly wrong and would be for months. Cars sat curbside, crushed by bricks broken from a nearby building or nearly impaled by a tree whose trunk was snapped like a matchstick. Trees and utility poles leaned toward streets, creating a canopy of sorts, OK to drive through if you sat comfortably in a military Humvee, but not in a rented Chevy Cavalier. Buildings had chunks carved out, as if someone took a bite out of the structures.

I kept asking myself what happened, even as we all knew the answer. I wondered if this wasn't the product of some prolonged neglect, the kind found in a Third World country. Some would agree, but only because the right people didn't heed published warnings about the levees being unable to withstand a storm of Katrina's strength.

It also had the look of a Hollywood set, meaning this couldn't possibly be real. Could it? I kept waiting for stage hands to walk up and push away huge sections of the city.

How is anyone going to calculate all the losses? Fifteen years ago, I lost nearly everything I owned in an apartment fire. Thinking I was responsible for the fire, the landlord of the eight-unit, stone mansion threatened to sue me for everything I had. I threw my shirt at him and told him, "Here, you can have half now." But what I lost were possessions and, temporarily, a home. Whether someone lost so much as a brick or all of their belongings,

EADS' JETTIES
Looking Seaward

ALF MAURSEN.Y.

people in the Gulf lost far more than I did. They are missing a sense of place that may never come back.

People who came to the Gulf, be it the military or the media—the most visible arrivals—quickly gained a small sense of the helplessness and isolation Katrina's victims felt. Getting out via cell was a hit or miss—and mostly miss—be it New Orleans or any of the Gulf areas affected by the storm. But on this late afternoon, I pushed two calls through. I first reached Michelle Williams, AP's Dallas-based Texas news editor. Next I got through to Adam Geller, a New York-based reporter who doubled as my editor that day.

They didn't know it at the time, but picking up the phone meant a lot more than discussing the next day's story or what day I'm coming home. It removed the distance that seemed far greater than one time zone or a two-hour flight.

Afterward, I pulled out my laptop, sat on a pile of bricks and began typing some thoughts about one of the city's unheralded features: the Port of New Orleans, the nation's largest importer of coffee, steel and rubber.

I'm not sure what street I was on because the sign was missing and there was no local person to answer that question. I think it was North Peters.

The port was my reason for coming to New Orleans, having already made stops in four Mississippi cities affected by Katrina. I was lucky to meet the port's director, Gary LaGrange, who upon introduction, extended his hand and said, "Welcome to Ground Zero."

Ask anyone who works at the port, and they'll tell you how subdued it had become. Flooding, spoiled produce and damaged coffee were just the surface changes. What was missing was the port acting as an intermodal nexus of movement among trucks, ships, barges and trains run by thousands of longshoremen, drivers, barge pilots and crew.

Before Katrina landed, the port was a warren of activity with cranes unloading cargo as fast as they were loading it—sometimes one item per minute—and trucks hitting the road. Cruise ships were unloading guests looking to extend their vacations in New Orleans' French Quarter, or they were picking up ship goers ready for a trip at sea.

But now the port's headquarters and some terminals along the river served as military and law enforcement bases established for relief and rescue efforts. Except for a few fourth-floor offices, LaGrange's office building was full of military personnel who seemed to have established permanence with stacks of supplies and cots set up throughout the lobby.

Outside the building, military personnel had pitched tents in parking lots and in port terminals. They patrolled the area heavily armed.

An aircraft carrier sat docked where LaGrange was accustomed to seeing ships from Carnival, Norwegian and Royal Caribbean cruise lines pulling up. The carrier served as headquarters for New Orleans Mayor Ray Nagin as well as home base for the choppers regularly lifting off to survey the area.

All of this against the backdrop of a serene sun beating down on the Mississippi River as if nothing had ever happened. LaGrange stood on the balcony outside of his office, looked outward, smiled and said, "I guess it's the calm after the storm. It really is beautiful out there."

Where Grace Lives.

TONI McGEE CAUSEY

I PASSED A MAN AT A SHELTER the other day. He was tall and lanky and sunburned, dressed in cut-offs and a soaked blue T-shirt with a grubby baseball cap shoved on top of muddy curls. There was something about his lean, sinewy body that made me think of the shrimpers I've seen down in Cocodrie, southwest of New Orleans—it's a hard life and it makes for no-nonsense, self-sufficient men.

He was sitting in a metal folding chair, slumped forward, his elbows on his knees. The exhaustion in his shoulders made me ache. Between his feet was a medium-sized box, and he was staring down into it. The box held some basic necessities: toiletries, canned goods, a pair of socks and a pair of underwear. I realized, then, that he was barefoot—the grime around his ankles marked him as having abandoned his shoes somewhere along the way. His large feet were probably too big for any of the donated shoes stacked up at one of the nearby tables.

When I looked back at that box, I wondered what he must be thinking. My first guess, without seeing his face, was that these few items weren't much to give a man after he'd lost everything. This box wasn't much to hold onto for a man like that, a man who'd clearly worked hard for a living. Maybe he was angry at having lost his home, or frustrated that this was what he'd been reduced to. I had no words that would be of use, no words which could do any good, and I began to turn away when he suddenly looked up and caught my eye.

He had tears on his cheeks.

When I stood there, not sure what to say, he shrugged and said, "I can't believe how generous people are. I can't believe total strangers would go out of their way to help so much."

I mumbled something about it being the least we could do, as neighbors, and I moved off into the crowd, feeling wholly inadequate and humbled in the face of such grace.

It would be one among many things I could not wrap my mind around.

On Tuesday morning, just a few days earlier, we'd been without electricity since Hurricane Katrina had blown through in the early hours of Monday. While there were many trees down in Baton Rouge, the damage wasn't as horrific as it had been during Hurricane Andrew, and we thought the worst was over.

It was only the beginning.

We managed to get our TV hooked to the generator and found one local station airing news and video from New Orleans. There was no way to know what images the national media were getting, but on Tuesday morning, I saw some of the first footage of one of the breaks in the levee system. Water was pouring into the Ninth Ward, and I felt all my senses hit hyper-alert, felt my fingers tingle from the adrenaline, felt my lungs constrict.

New Orleans was filling up.

At first, it appeared that no one nationally realized what was happening. After plugging the computer into the generator as well and discovering I still had DSL, I caught bits and pieces on national websites saying things like "New Orleans dodged the bullet." There was a steady thrum of "no no no no no" in my head, an awful, gut-kick ache, a sense of the world gone topsy. With the water pouring in, the levees were going to keep deteriorating. The pressure from the flow of water was simply going to be too great.

The pumps were already down in some areas, and more were failing. Saying "New Orleans had dodged a bullet" was the clearest sign that the outside media didn't grasp what was happening. It was a bit like telling a terminal cancer patient that they "only" had a broken arm (i.e., wind damage, some minor flooding); it doesn't matter, the cancer's going to kill them anyway before the arm can heal. New Orleans was already suffering from the worst kind of cancer—years of inadequate repairs to the levees (or no repairs at all), years of talking about a plan to evacuate, years of warnings that a plan was going to be needed, years of awareness that New Orleans was a bowl and if it filled up, it could be devastating. I remember being on the phone with a friend in L.A. as fresh images of the ever-increasing deluge from the levees hit the local news. The chill I felt, I cannot explain. I remember saying, "Ohmygod, we're going to lose New Orleans."

And we did.

There are images which will crush me and haunt me forever. Moments seared into my heart. Entire neighborhoods under water, many with just the topmost part of the roofs visible. People clinging to the peak of what had been their homes in desperation, some for days on end, with no water, no food, no help and little hope. An elderly woman trying to talk her mentally handicapped son into climbing on board the basket being lowered by the Coast Guard Rescue Team, and him refusing unless she came, too. But there was room for only one. He wouldn't go, and she couldn't leave him behind. There was the image of a mother trapped on a rooftop, handing over her small toddler to the Coast Guard, and the news helicopter showing her breaking down as the Coast Guard helicopter flew away; they'd only had room for one more, and she wanted her child saved. People stood on their roofs, waving to the helicopters, desperate to be rescued, only to see the helicopters leave since they were full. I remember the image of two men standing in shock on their own roof, watching a home near them burn, knowing the fire department could do nothing to stop it from spreading.

There are images and moments which scarred us all, embedded deep somewhere in our souls, a slash that will not heal. The sights and sounds of people abandoned, dying, here on our soil. There's the crystal image for me of the late night DJ for a New Orleans radio station breaking down as he reported on air on a Baton Rouge TV station how he'd been up all night, broadcasting in New Orleans. He told of how his station still had a signal locally, though no one could explain it when so many others had been knocked off the air, and how he realized that the police didn't have any communication system at all. People were calling in to him, a few cellphones still working. They were begging for help because they were trapped in their homes, trapped in their attics. When he realized neither they nor he had a way to call the police, he'd broadcast the addresses and hope the police heard him so the trapped people would get help.

The DJ told of one call: a young woman who was holding her infant. She had a two-year-old with her, and her elderly grandmother. They had not evacuated because they had no car to enable them to leave and no place to stay. They were standing chest deep in water, in her attic, and no way to break through the roof, no way to alert police where they were. Her cellphone died before the DJ could get her address to broadcast her location. He never knew if they were rescued.

There were the talk-radio stories from the frustrated and grief-stricken men who'd responded to the call for boats, any boats, and they'd gone to the designated areas, fully prepared to take on the responsibility for any damage they received—they didn't care, they just wanted to save lives. They weren't allowed into the water for a full day due to a series of miscommunications between various government agencies. There were the harrowing stories of having to pass people up because their boats were already full, of the boat operators promising to go back, and then doing so, only for the person to have died or vanished. There were the voices in the dark, a night so deep where no light penetrated, where streetlights and businesses and every imaginable source was out and the voices cried from the rooftops, pleading for help.

There are the now-infamous images of the way people were abandoned at the Superdome and the Convention Center; people forced to go days without food, water, basic human needs. People sick and dying. No help in sight. No organization, no FEMA, no Red Cross in many places. There were the images of the looting and the crime. People reduced to the base animal instincts, some for survival, some to prey on others.

Nothing but dying and suffering in the Big Easy.

Our world changed, then. Shelters went up in every available space: churches, synagogues, and in the River Center, an entertainment complex in downtown Baton Rouge. Other states took in many thousands, and yet, thousands more were here. Everything was different. Even places as old and forever as LSU.

When you drive up Nicholson onto the southern end of the LSU campus, rising to your right is the enormous stadium (under even more expansion), with its parking lot a construction laydown yard. To the left, Alex Box Stadium, with all of the national championships proclaimed proudly on the exterior walls.

If you looked a little past the stadium on the right, you'd see the Pete Maravich Center, or P-MAC for short. (It's what many of us old LSU grads still refer to simply as the "Assembly" Center.) Its white dome and curved concrete ramps will always hold a special place in my heart—it's where I officially became an LSU student, years ago. Back before there was computer registration, we all "walked through," battling and jockeying in lines on the floor of the Center to claim a punch card for the class we wanted—a slender three-by-seven card with chads punched out, indicating the class for which we'd just enrolled. We'd take the cards and climb to the second level and walk around the mezzanine's corridor, stopping at the various tables set up for each task required and then, finally, on to pay our fee bill.

It was exciting to be a part of that crowd. It was fresh, it was hope, it was a beginning into all potential. It was a promise of something bigger to come.

After the hurricane, we drove onto campus and parked in the Alex Box parking lot, took the crosswalk and headed back toward the P-MAC. There was the white dome gleaming in spite of being overshadowed by the behemoth stadium. There was the newly renovated Mike-the-Tiger cage, a luxurious enclosure complete with rocks to climb, a waterfall, a very large pool and plenty of space to run and play. Next came the concrete ramps which had long ago made me feel like I had been racing up up up toward a future.

Then there was the fence.

A fence.

There had never been a hurricane fence preventing access to the ramps. Or military standing outside said fence. So around the P-MAC we went, getting to the LSU campus side, making a sharp left turn to walk up the street. There was a large white poster-board sign on the guard's gate in hastily written print which said "Ambulances" and had an arrow.

The P-MAC was still on our left, and as I looked across the fence and beneath the mezzanine, there were tables set up. This time, though, it was not like before, when I registered there, when the tables were about hope and future and innocent dreams. These tables were about loss and devastation and pain. There were volunteers behind the tables and many evacuees in front, having just gotten in from New Orleans. There was a table set up with laptops so the people could send a message. There were tables of clothes and shoes (which ran out just as soon as the volunteers could get some in), tables of water and food to eat right then, as well as canned goods and other supplies for the evacuees to take with them ... for many of them hoped to bunk with family for the night, and that family probably didn't even know they were coming.

As we continued around the P-MAC, I could tell we were reaching the serious part of this operation, where there were nurses and techs taking medical information, where higher priority (read: in grave danger) patients were taken in immediately to the triage center and where those in dire need but with less life-threatening conditions were interviewed by nurses, their stats recorded on brand new files. Nurses and doctors and all sorts of techs ebbed and flowed through this space. There were guards with guns (wholly overkill, but they were there). There were volunteers of all shapes and sizes—from LSU and Southern students to firemen to police to little grey-haired church ladies.

We signed in at the non-medical volunteer station and went in to see what their needs were. We were there to volunteer our home to medical staff. We'd heard the staff were working twenty-hour shifts and some of them had no place nearby to just crash and relax.

When you walked inside the entrance, you walked down a slight slope until you reached the wide, round base of the P-MAC. Purple seating had been pushed up against the walls. The last time I stood at floor level like that, I was seventeen, and I remember I stood for a moment in awe of the swarm of people, the organized chaos, the feeling of a small city set to work on one task. It was, in many ways, the same. But this time, that small city was made of dozens of white temporary screens to give the patients some privacy, and many rows of IV bags.

There was a MASH unit on my campus. A field unit triage on the floor of our basketball arena. There were helicopters beating overhead bringing in evacuees from New Orleans, and a row of ambulances, sirens blaring, on their way to the P-MAC.

There was a MASH unit. In Louisiana. In my university.

In the USA.

It simply didn't seem possible, that there would be this necessity. That we had so many people wounded in a major catastrophe, that we lost an entire city, that we were still finding and rescuing people, six days later—so many people that our hospitals and clinics were swamped, and a major triage unit was not only critical, but it barely handled the vast quantity of people flowing in.

So many unbelievable things were suddenly true. Families couldn't find loved ones. People without their medicines, without any identification, tried to remember what they needed so the nurses could help them. A mom cried with gratitude because she found someone's cast-off clothes to fit her children. Others, tears streaming, were just grateful to have their own bar of soap, or a bottle of water.

In the USA.

It was at the LSU triage where I met the man without the shoes, the shrimper who was grateful for a small box of goods. He was sitting beneath the mezzanine, just next to the ramps where I'd walked up up up into the hope of a better future all those years ago. I turned away, knowing his future was going to be difficult and painful, and maybe so much worse.

Everything had changed.

We lost New Orleans and many many homes surrounding it. How can we understand that?

The business of surviving, or more accurately, of trying to help a huge number of other people survive, took over for many of us who live here. We exchanged information about where there were needs, we gathered what we could, we brought it wherever we could. We met families all staying in one home, forty-five people in a thousand-square-foot house, sleeping in borrowed tents in the yard, wearing nothing but the clothes they'd escaped with. We heard so many stories of people who lost everything, who had no clue if there was going to be a New Orleans to go back to, if their job would still exist, if there would be a school for their children. In the midst of the pain, they would often get a faraway expression in their gaze, like they were looking off to some memory of New Orleans, and then they'd look at one another and say, "But we got out. We're all OK. At least we're alive."

We lost New Orleans.

My family and I walked into places where there were so many trees and utilities down on the ground, you couldn't tell a street from a yard. Signposts were missing, homes were destroyed, one after another. We stepped over power lines, and visited homes of friends' families, looking for survivors.

We lost New Orleans.

The heartbreak kept me from sleeping, and I'm not entirely sure I ate anything remotely resembling a proper meal for days. It was grief, I know, so I did the only real thing I knew how to do: I wrote. I poured it into a blog, and many people would post notes about missing loved ones, and others were begging for any information at all about their neighborhoods. These notes chased me in my dreams, always just below the surface. The helplessness etched into every waking moment, acid into the pores, and rendered the grief unbelievably deep.

We lost New Orleans.

A few days into the disaster, many more boxes showed up here with supplies. More and more people wrote to ask what we needed. More and more people were as outraged and frustrated as we were here, and they wanted to help. I know many donated to charities, but these boxes—they kept showing up, filled to the brim with things people needed, with supplies damned near impossible to find in some of these areas. We got to bring them to the shelters and to the people who needed them, and the recipients treated me like a hero, but it was not me. It was you. It was every single one of you who sent a box or a prayer or letters of support.

I don't know how to explain the effect these supplies had. There was the immediate help, of course. So many things were needed by so many people. Baton Rouge doubled in size from evacuees, and for those who could get to the stores, they were crowded and often stripped of goods. I saw clerks stocking shelves only to have items plucked out of their hands before they could even set them down. I had to go to four or five stores sometimes to find things that were needed. And while it was helpful and useful and much required, all of these supplies, it was more than that.

MADAME JOHN'S LEGACY

It was the message that we're not alone.

The rage I felt watching New Orleans drown is still palpable. I cannot understand the fact that we live in a country which can put men on the moon, which can help build an international space station, which can create phenomenal structures or explore the deepest oceans, but we could not get water to people trapped on an overpass for days. I cannot wrap my mind around why they were trapped in the first place, since there were trucks passing them by. FEMA trucks, which wouldn't stop. I don't understand that. And I can't believe I live in a country which could show this on TV, for days in a row, and no one did anything about it.

New Orleans was dying. People were dying. It was just one scene of so many, and it made no sense. People died on that overpass, when help just drove right by them.

I cannot understand how media crews could show the devastating events down at the Convention Center and the Superdome, and FEMA or our federal government did not "know" the people were there. How do we live in a country which can drop aid to everyone else in the world, and no one could drop water and food to the people trapped there? How can we handle going into war-torn areas and get aid to people there, but a few thugs prevented us from helping Americans? How?

How is it that more than two weeks later when we were still going to shelters bringing in supplies, I received reports from the outlying areas that FEMA still hadn't shown up?

Still. Hadn't. Shown. Up.

I don't understand these things. I know I live in America. Well, last time I checked, Louisiana was still in America. New Orleans was still a major American city. Maybe something happened somewhere that someone forgot to mention to us, but yeah, pretty sure we're still in America. And the magnitude of the inept response (including local government) was staggering.

It was like watching someone I love get gutted and lie there bleeding and knowing that help was standing a few feet away, talking about golf scores.

So when I say to you that you've made a difference, I don't mean it lightly or in any sort of frivolous way. When it suddenly became clear that we were the ugly, unwanted stepchild of the government, or worse, the beaten, neglected child of the local officials who were hastily trying to cover up their long-term abuse with loud excuses, you made us feel human again. So many of you—giving, calling, writing, trying. Feeling the outrage on our behalf. Knowing it belonged to you, because you were us, we were a part of this country, and you cared.

We lost New Orleans. We needed you, and you were there, and the outpouring of that grace and hope helped to get us through the worst of the days when we were watching in horror as our own people died, as our friends and family were left, as people were treated worse than we'd ever *ever* treat an animal.

You made a difference. A big difference. And we thank you.

*If you ever witnessed a funeral in New Orleans
and they have one of those brass bands playing
this funeral, you really have a bunch of musicians
playing from the heart, because as they go to the
cemetery they play in a funeral march, they play
"Flee as a Bird," "Nearer my God Today," and they
express themselves in those instruments singing
those notes the same as a singer would, you know.
And they take this body to the cemetery and
they put this body in the ground. While he's doin'
that the snare drummer takes the handkerchief
from under the drum, from under the snare, and
they say "ashes to ashes" and put him away and
everything, and the drummer rolls up the drum
real loud. And outside the cemetery they form and
they start swinging "Didn't He Ramble." And all
the members, the Oddfellows, whatever lodge it
is, they are on this side. And on this [other] side
is a bunch of raggedy guys, you know, old hustlers
and cats and good-time Charlies and everything.
Well, they right with the parade too. And when
they get to wailin' this "Didn't He Ramble" and
finish, seems as though they have more fun than
anybody, because they applaud for Joe Oliver and
Manny Perez, with the brass band, to play it over
again, so they got to give this second line, they call
it, an encore. So that makes them have a lot of
fun, too, and it's really something to see.*

— LOUIS ARMSTRONG,
interviewed by EDWARD R. MURROW
in the film *Satchmo the Great*

THE RETURN

Oh! Didn't he ramble, ramble,
He rambled all around, in and out of town;
Oh! Didn't he ramble, ramble,
He rambled till the butchers cut him down.

Listen to the Second Line.

COLLEEN MONDOR

HERE'S THE TRUTH, the embarrassing truth: I have never been to New Orleans.

What I know about the city, what I love about it, is almost completely based on music. I am not a music authority, just a music lover and everywhere that I have lived (from Florida to Alaska and now the Pacific Northwest), New Orleans music has been a constant. It is part of my first musical memory; it's present in the saddest moment of my life and, in one way or another, it is what I turn to more than any other sound. New Orleans is not my city, but its music is certainly what I know best; its music is most definitely mine.

When I was growing up, my mother played her old forty-fives on Saturdays while cleaning house. Standing in the living room, dancing to 1950s rock and roll, we would crowd in front of the fans and drink Kool-Aid out of plastic cups. It is always hot in Florida when you don't have air conditioning, and my mother's records were often the only thing that kept us moving. That little house on a sleepy two-lane road is where I learned about Elvis, Sam Cooke and Johnny Mathis. It's also the first time I heard Fats Domino.

Singing with my mom to "Blueberry Hill" and "Ain't That

a Shame" is where my musical memory begins. And although I spent years wandering around the rock and pop landscape (I did grow up in the eighties after all; forgive me my Madonna fascination), I have never forgotten the booming sound of Fats Domino filling our living room. When you grow up, you figure out fast what you like and what you don't, and his sound was one I wanted more of. The surprise for me though was that Domino's sound was just one of many coming from New Orleans. Domino's hometown, unlike so many other places, does not hold tightly to one sound. It is not Nashville, or Detroit or even Memphis. Rather it is simply the city where music has a place to begin. More than any other, it is a place of musical possibility, and because of that, an endless source of stunning collaborations.

I think part of the reason why Louisiana music appeals to me so much is the rich history that permeates the landscape. Growing up in Florida, I learned early that nothing is sacred, not even the Everglades. I have seen every inch of my hometown changed by condos and strip malls and no amount of writing by John D. MacDonald or Carl Hiaasen is ever going to expose all the ways in which the land has been destroyed. The saddest thing for me though is the total and complete loss of the area's history. Other than the fort at St. Augustine and a few other outposts, Florida is strictly an altar to discount shopping and plastic design. Even the orange groves are disappearing. We like Wal-Mart a lot in my hometown; hell, we practically worship it.

The truth is, history doesn't live long in Florida, not unless it's courtesy one of Walt Disney's animatronic shows.

My hometown has been so transformed that it is barely recognizable, and maybe that is why I love the sounds of Louisiana. When you listen to Cajun music, you are hearing tunes that date back to the Acadians in Nova Scotia, Creole music echoes the songs of Caribbean immigrants and jazz recalls the field-hand hollers in the decades after the Civil War. In reality though, no one knows for certain how any one of these song styles evolved in the manner in which they did. How did Anthony Maggio take cries from the cotton fields and men in Southern chain gangs in 1907 and transform them into the earliest published blues song, "I Got the Blues?" What prompted the blending of marching band music, ragtime, blues and gospel to start a jazz revolution in Storyville that has been heard around the world? How did they all become so fearless in their reaches for new sounds and yet so loyal to the region's history at the same time? What kind of place encourages such risk takers and yet demands and receives a respect for the past? Is it some kind of luck that just passed other places by, but gave Buddy Bolton, Jelly Roll Morton and King Oliver the spark they needed to set the music on fire? Can that be only luck?

Must it be magic?

Or maybe it's just that no one else was listening when the songs were born in the fields and bars and jump shacks. Maybe no one else noticed and that's why most of us are still standing outside, pretending to understand; a bunch of tourists who couldn't possibly know what lives and breathes in these sounds or anticipate what might come next.

Maybe that's why we just listen while the people who live there, who immerse themselves in the atmosphere, are the ones who make the music.

* * *

Louis Armstrong was from New Orleans, along with Wynton and Branford Marsalis, Mahalia Jackson, the Neville Brothers, Harry Connick Jr., Dr. John, Professor Longhair, soul singer Irma Thomas and the multitalented Allen Toussaint. Memphis Minnie grew up there as well and contributed her own prescient sound to the city's history when she wrote "When the Levee Breaks" with Kansas Joe McCoy way back in 1929. In the areas surrounding the city, you find Mark and Ann Savoy keeping Cajun music alive; Sonny Landreth speaking volumes with his

CREOLE SONGS.

From *Historical Sketch Book and Guide to New Orleans*, New Orleans Press, 1885.

The following Creole song was popular in Louisiana at the beginning of the century:

Moin pas conne qui quichose	Toi conne qui belle rigole
Qui appe tourmente moin la;	Qui coule dans bananiers,
Moin pas conne qui la cause,	Ou toi te si fe la folle
Cœur a moin brule comme ça.	La foi qui toi te baigne,
Ah Die! Qui tourment, qui peine,	D'leau la pas coule encore,—
Dipis longtemps quimbe moi;	Des fois li 'rete tout court,—
C'este tourment la passe chaine,	Li semble regrette encore
Plutot moin mouri youne fois	Li pas baigne toi toujours.

Here is a free translation:

I do not know what it is which torments me thus.
I can not tell what it is that makes my heart beat so.
O God! what torture! what pains I have suffered so long!
It is worse than the pain of fetters; I had rather die at once.

Do you remember the pretty little brook that ran through the banana trees—
Where you used to have such fun, when you used to bathe?
That water has ceased to run;—
Since the time it stopped all at once—
It seems to me it died of regret
That its wavelets could not embrace you forever.

* * * * *

Another Popular Creole song:

Z'autres qu'a di moin, ca yon bonheur;	Others say, it is your happiness;
Et moin va di, ca yon peine;—	I say, it is your sorrow;
D'amour quand porte la chaine,	When we are enchanted by love,
Adieu, courri tout bonheur!	Farewell to all happiness!
Pauvre piti' Mamzel Zizi!	Poor little Miss Zizi!
Pauvre piti' Mamzel Zizi!	Poor little Miss Zizi!
Pauvre piti' Mamzel Zizi!	Poor little Miss Zizi!
Pauvre piti' Mamzel Zizi!	Poor little Miss Zizi!
Li gagnin doulor, doulor, doulor,—	She has sorrow, sorrow, sorrow;—
Li gagnin doulor dans cœur a li!	She has sorrow in her heart.

* * * * *

The following is a remnant of a song which must be considerably over a century old, and which used to be sung by the blacks on the plantations in the early days of the century:

Di tems Misslé d'Artaguette,	In the days of d'Artaguette,
Hé! Ho! Hé!	. Hé! Ho! Hé!
C'était, c'était bon tems,	It was the good old time,
Yé té ménin monde à la baguette,	The world was led straight with a switch,
Hé! Ho! Hé!	Hé! Ho! Hé!
Pas negrès, pas rubans,	There were no negros,
Pas diamans,	No diamonds,
Pour Dochans,	For the vulgar,
Hé! Ho! Hé!	Hé! Ho! Hé!

guitar; and Marcia Ball wailing on the piano with a wicked Texas and Louisiana swing that is a new definition of joy. Keith Frank has lately taken zydeco to new heights, giving the Creole blending with rhythm and blues a wider audience than it has seen before. Marc Broussard is a modern soul and rock combination from the small town of Carenco, and Jolie Holland has her own Crescent City back porch sound that has reached all the way to Canada and influenced the British Columbia groups Be Good Tanyas and Po' Girl, both of whom have written songs honoring the New Orleans music tradition.

Perhaps the music travels so well because its roots are interwoven so thoroughly into the fabric of New Orleans. There are simply no boundaries, both musically and geographically, for the New Orleans and Southern Louisiana sound; there is only the music, and all the musicians who willingly embrace it.

Armstrong is, of course, the one who put the city on the map. My sentimental favorite of his many songs is "What a Wonderful World," strictly because it never fails to make me feel hopeful about the future. His gravelly voice, hiding its own secret smile, is unmistakable, and whether singing the stories of "Mack the Knife," and "Frankie and Johnny" or holding court on life back home in "Do You Know What It Means to Miss New Orleans?" he owns the room that his songs are played in and sets a mood that cannot be ignored. He is credited with popularizing the Dixieland sound that is prevalent in many aspects of New Orleans life, most directly for his arrangement of "When the Saints Go Marching In." Before Armstrong presented the song as part of the Reverend Satchmo's "mock jazz church" in May 1938 for Decca Records, it was known as a gospel tune of unknown origin, although the general consensus is that it dates to the African-American spirituals so prevalent in the South. Armstrong added some brass and sass and dropped most of the verses. Ultimately he created a boisterous challenge to death, an insistence that even when it comes to funerals, the people of New Orleans would sing their way to the graveyards. I think

Armstrong would agree though that in the wake of Hurricane Katrina, his ecstatic version of the song was misplaced in concerts for the city. I reached instead for Dr. John's return to the song's gospel roots, a haunting and soulful rendition with Mavis Staples that reminds the listener the singer is begging to be remembered. What could be more appropriate in those first stunning days after the storm than a plea to be "included in that golden number," a prayer not to be left behind. This is the song for places we will never forget: the Superdome, the Convention Center, the desperate stretch of Highway I-10. "We'll all be reunited on a new and distant shore," according to the lyrics; eventually, perhaps, for the lucky ones.

Gospel has long been a part of Southern Louisiana music with Mahalia Jackson as only one of literally thousands who began their careers in parish churches. Dr. John weaves the city's religious roots in and out of his music, pairing songs as divergent as "Lay My Burden Down" alongside the homage to Voodoo Queen Marie Laveau on his CD *N'awlinz Dis Dat or D'udda*. It works there as well as it works in the cemeteries and the message is clear: worshipping your God is your business as long as the singing is done with style.

The Neville Brothers have certainly been influenced by gospel, and when they join together they are as likely to present a song that belongs in a church as a civil rights march. What drew me to them years ago was their protest music, the way they applied their own sensitive harmonies both to songs written by Bob Dylan and Sam Cooke as well as their own anthems such as "Sister Rosa" and "Wake Up." Their revolutionary spirit is still going strong in their latest CD, along with the unique brand of funk that only the Nevilles seem able to supply. It is the words that carry an undeniable sense of urgency in their music, however, the lyrics that take precedence. And listening to Aaron Neville sing those words is what I consider a religious experience—the religion of equality and justice as well as faith in God.

Aaron Neville has a version of the Randy Newman song "Louisiana 1927" that was largely unknown until Katrina. Newman spent his childhood summers with family in New Orleans and credits those years as the impetus to study the city's history. His research culminated in the Flood of 1927 and the fateful decision by the city fathers back then to persuade the Corps of Engineers to dynamite a levee to the south and relieve pressure on the New Orleans flood controls. The city was saved but Evangeline Parish paid the price. As Newman wrote:

> *The river has busted through clear down to Plaquemines*
> *Six feet of water in the streets of Evangeline*

What escapes most listeners is that the mournful chorus,

> *Louisiana, Louisiana*
> *They're tryin' to wash us away*
> *They're tryin' to wash us away*

is not about the river but about the people who diverted the flood so the poor paid the highest price. Almost seventy years later, the same questions raised by Newman could be heard by Americans everywhere, as the country struggled to understand how so many people could be left behind to face the flooded streets of New Orleans. Neville's version of "Louisiana 1927" makes me cry every time I hear it, and lately, I have been playing it again and again.

By its very nature, the music of New Orleans often inspires a gut response among its listeners. As it is based so heavily in the voices of those who lost everything, in the memories of the Acadians, the African Americans, in the poor of all races and the hopeless of every class, it commands a circumspect moment from those who seek it out. It appeals to listeners across all boundaries of color and class, however, and does not know a generational division. It is most completely the music of the people, a universal sound that Wynton Marsalis attributes to its jazz roots as much as anything else. "Jazz is important," writes Marsalis, "because it's the only art form that embodies the fundamental principles of American democracy."

It is the most American of music then, the sounds that tell us who we are and thus what it means to be an American at all.

* * *

Several years ago, I listened to Louis Armstrong sing day after day as I watched my father die. He would smile, barely conscious, when he heard Armstrong's voice. I did not know until those days, those miserable dark days, that my father and I had this music in common, that we could have talked about New Orleans and jazz and blues in all the years that led us to those final moments together. I told him I loved Armstrong while I sat beside him and I think he understood; I hope he did. It gives me a shared memory if he knew; it gives me one more way to remember him.

I know that the music of New Orleans will survive any catastrophe; the records are set, the lyrics transcribed, the recordings known all over the world. It can never disappear. But the magic of that place is not in the music it already knows, but in the sounds that are yet to be. The Acadians who came there in 1755 could never have imagined that one day their influence would be heard in something called jazz, and the Southern conscripts in nineteenth century work camps would never believe their mournful calls would collide with other sounds and produce the blues. The city has already played witness to an evolution in musical styles that is without precedent in our collective human memory. What I want to hear though, is what comes next. New Orleans is not done yet, not by a long shot. I want to hear what she has to give us next.

A Creole Court-Yard ⚜ Royal Street

A Lesson from Below.

SARAH K. INMAN

"Priorities: A hundred years from now it will not matter what my bank account was, the sort of house I lived in, or the kind of car I drove ... but the world may be different because I was important in the life of a child."

— from a poster on sale in a SkyMall catalog

THE PEAK OF YOUR TRAPEZE PERFORMING career has passed, but still you go two or three times a week to the warehouse where the apparatus hangs. You train because occasionally you get called to revel, to dance up high for conventioneers. You go out of habit, out of the need to stay in shape and to hang upside down, believing that inversion is a crucial part of your mental well-being. The warehouse is located in the Marigny area of downtown New Orleans, not far from the River, not far from the train tracks and all their symbolism. The space itself is called the ARK, and it's a place for artists, politicos and bohemians. Even though you have a full-time job, you see yourself connected to these people, if only by space and the fact that you also voted the Kerry/Edwards ticket. In addition to the aerial equipment, there's a book collective that specializes in zines and writings of a political persuasion. From the trapeze, you can look down into the Iron Rail Book Collective and see a red flag with a black sickle, the shelves of books and magazines, the couch and end table that make the place a small comfort.

The ARK is also home to Project B, or the Bicycle Project, another collective of people, but these people deal with bikes, not books. They collect parts of bicycles and build, repair and sell them. Project B rests in the back of the warehouse, out of your view, and on most days you can hear the people playing music as they work. Sometimes there's a pounding or the noise of an electric tool being used. As far as you know, anyone is welcome to Project B. The organization even boasts a night devoted to women and transvestites who want to work on their bikes free from men and the patriarchal bullshit their presence imposes, and on weekends and weekday afternoons, the space attracts its fair share of local schoolchildren.

At one time the ARK housed a theater. Part of the walls and ceiling are still painted black from a performance of "The House of Yes" that was produced almost two years ago. At another time—not too long ago—there were computers with Internet access available for the youth who found themselves here. But for now the rest of the warehouse is filled with storage from someone's costume shop. When you reach the top of the rope or stand on the bar of the trapeze, you can look out and see rows of Mardi Gras costumes, their shiny fabric adding a much needed glow to the dark place. There are boxes of pink and silver King Kong get-ups and bear suits, cat suits and headdresses. There are accessories, capes and caps, wigs and tiaras and props, bows and arrows, fake swords and guns, too, nestled in half-closed boxes.

One Saturday afternoon, after a long morning of writing and grading, the sitting down kind of activities that your spine demands release from, you head to the ARK to train.

Training alone is never wise and you know this, but there just aren't many aerialists in town. So you go alone, knowing better, and the usual crowd is there at the Iron Rail Book Collective: the skinny punky girl with dyed black hair cut into an asymmetrical shape; the muscular guy with the Mohawk and pierced septum, the one who calls himself Moose and writes poetry; the dreadlocked blonde-headed girl with a tiny tattoo on her forehead. You think she goes by the name Bruhau. They are there, engaged in dialogue, doing book collective stuff. There are a few strangers, as always, and on this particular Saturday, there are children. At first you just hear them, their chatter booming through the warehouse. The volume of their voices suggests an energy that needs to be released. They're curious and hungry for activity. They are waiting for Project B to open.

For a while the feeble partitions separate you from them. You listen to them prattle on, asking the book collective people when the bike project will open and asking them for stuff they can have for free. "I can have this tape?" a voice asks.

"It's not mine to give, little man," a guy responds.

"I can borrow it then?" the boy asks.

"I don't know you that well."

You spread out your mats and stretch, knowing that sooner or later your activity will no longer be a secret because once you climb the rope and get on the trapeze, once you're higher than those little walls, everyone will see you, at least anyone who is looking up.

You are reluctant to get up on the bar, knowing that the children will want to watch, or even more likely, try out the trapeze. You want to avoid this whole situation, but you stretch for some time, and your muscles are ready for exercise. It's your day off. You're not wearing a watch. You don't know how long before Project B opens and the kids will be occupied with other things. You grab the bar of the trapeze, beat to your knees and hang for a moment, enjoying the blood rushing to the brain. Then you slide your elbows under the bar, grip the lines, tuck and roll to sitting, a move called the double monkey roll or Russian roll, depending on where you learned circus skills. You begin with some basic static moves like bananas—one leg stretched straight along the bar, the other bent into the line, the upper body hanging down from one side of the trapeze—and laybacks—one hand gripping the line while legs press into the opposite line, the body arching out. No sooner are you up there, visible from above the partition, than you hear, "Ooo, how you get there?" It comes from the other side of the divide; one of the little boys has spotted you, and now all four little men are staring up at you on the trapeze. The boys wear T-shirts and baggy jeans or shorts. It's warm for November, and there are two bikes between them.

"Climbed," you answer. A stringy-haired young woman sits on the couch outside the book collective talking with a guy you've never seen before. He has a deep voice, and he seems to be giving her legal advice. He acknowledges your presence by nodding, and you respond with a "how you doing?"

"How?" one little boy shouts back at you. His hair is a tight little Afro. He cannot be older than ten.

"I can climb this rope or jump up," you say, but you realize you have misunderstood him.

"No, how you get over there?" he asks.

"Back here," another boy answers and begins to do just that, race around the partition that separates your training space from the book collective and the entrance to the ARK. Your space is no longer yours, your secret revealed. Three other boys follow in a great rush. They are local kids and they are black. It's been four years since you've started teaching at a community college whose student body is mostly nonwhite, and you've stopped fearing black people, except, of course, for the occasional lone soldier who pops up near your driveway past dark.

The boys run around the corner, wheeling their low-rider bikes. They scramble to the area where the trapeze and rope hang. One boy, the one whose pants are too long to be shorts but too short to be pants, runs toward the rope, grips it and swings. You yell at him for wearing shoes on your mat, the one from your brother's dojo, the one he gave you when you moved to the South and began this business. The boy kicks off his sneakers, and the others do the same. You warn them of how dangerous it is, of how they must take responsibility for themselves and their actions. You sound like your mother. "No, like this. Be careful. Not like that. You be careful." As much as you don't want to be like that, you cannot help but realize that the tone is needed.

They half hear your voice as they clamor for the rope. They take turns trying to climb all the way to the fifteen-foot ceiling. When they get close to the bar of the trapeze, with its decorative end jutting out, you tell them to watch their heads. The ends are made of steel. You stay on the trapeze, alternately doing tricks and hollering at the boys to keep them in check. You answer questions:

"How long you been doing this?"

"About five years."

"Does it hurt?"

"Yes."

They talk excitedly among themselves and tease one another; after all, rope climbing can be a simple contest of male strength. "How can I get up there?" One boy wants to play on the trapeze.

"You are not allowed." On this, you must be firm. It is, after all, a liability. You watch as the boys grasp the rope and desperately try to make their way to the top, using all arm strength and grunts. It's just not going to work like that. To climb a rope efficiently, you need to use your legs and core strength along with your arms. Still, two of the boys get about halfway to the ceiling before deciding to ditch their efforts and just let go, landing heavily on all fours on the mat. You warn them of the dangers of letting go.

"You got a boyfriend?" one of them asks. He's a little older than the other three, the boy who leads the way.

"I have a husband," you say. You try to make it sound more interesting than having a boyfriend.

After watching a few more daring leaps from rope to mat, you become nervous for their safety and tired of their antics. As politely and as firmly as you can, you tell them that rope time has ended. You need your space to train. To your surprise, they follow your command, but they leave their bikes near the mats and run off in dirty socks or bare feet, leaving their sneakers behind too.

Soon they are into the costumes and the boxes of props. They find the toy guns, and from high on the lines of the trapeze, you watch them shoot at you. You think about the young black men, in some cases not many years older than these kids, whom you read about in the paper, the ones who die of gunshot wounds inflicted by other young black men. How many more years before these kids find real weapons?

"I'm a kill you," one boy shouts.

"No, I got you." Now they are shooting at each other.

They came here to work on bikes. They came to practice a skill, a constructive one that involves their hands and their minds and their attention, and they arrived early, too early. And here you are just fucking around on your trapeze, staying in shape, clearing your head, getting your spinal release. Who are you to deny them a few moments of your attention, of your time? You've been thinking about volunteering to coach a girls' softball or basketball team or being a big sister. You've been thinking about these things, but you haven't acted on any of your intentions. Above the din of the fake automatic weapons, you call out, "All right. Let's have a quick lesson in rope climbing."

No sooner do you speak than they drop their guns and run back to the mats. "Me first," the little one with the Afro and rolled up jeans says.

"How old are y'all?" you ask, even though you've got plenty of nephews and nieces and have a sense of kids' ages. You guess they are around ten or eleven.

"I'm in the ninth grade," the tallest one offers. True, he is the tallest boy, but he doesn't seem like a ninth grader to you.

Perhaps it is the immaturity of the other boys that makes him appear younger than he claims.

"He's in the sixth grade, and he's in fifth; he's in the fourth grade," the tall boy answers for them all. Then a fifth child arrives, young like a fourth grader. He too is eager to climb this thing. You tell him to take his shoes off.

"Y'all have a rope in gym class?" you ask.

"Yeah, but I can't climb it cause I got too much stuff in my pants," the oldest boy says.

You ignore this comment for the benefit of the boys who want to learn.

You begin your lesson, first by demonstrating. "Wrap a leg around the rope and then reach as high as you can. Now, in one motion, as you tuck your wrapped leg into your chest, place your other foot on the sole of the wrapped foot and haul your whole body up. Keep squeezing with your legs and reach high with your hands. It's like you coil and straighten; move your hands up and then do it again."

They comment on your strength. You ask them about their favorite sports.

"I like football," the second oldest says.

"Football," repeats the fourth grader.

"Football and basketball," the other little one says.

"I like football," says the tall boy. He does pretty well on the rope. Though he doesn't use the coiling method you suggest, he figures out a way to use his toes to aid his climb.

"Great," you say when he reaches the top. He slides halfway down before jumping to the mat. "Careful." You are stern. You hold the bottom of the rope for the smaller boys, because having a little weight on the end can help make the climb easier. When you get around to holding the rope for the fifth grader, you can't help but notice he has an erection. You are kneeling on the mat, gripping the loose end of the rope, holding it taut for him. His crotch is eye level. You don't acknowledge it, nor does he. He simply climbs. You've talked with men about their erections and understand they can occur when there's rubbing, and yes, there is rubbing involved in rope climbing. You often leave the warehouse with rope burns on odd parts of your body, your inner thighs included. You think about what a college friend once said when she imagined what it would be like to be a guy. It would be tough having that thing, that uncontrollable thing, prone to random and sometimes inexplicable arousal. Once the boy reaches the top, you release your grip on the rope. Holding it isn't necessary for the climb down. When the boy reaches the mat again, his friend, the tall, older boy says, "For sports, I like having sex."

He's come in a little late with his joke. Your conversation of who liked what sports has passed.

"Well," you say. "Having sex can be an athletic activity." You will not laugh or be shocked or mad.

"Psych," he says gleefully, even though no one was psyched, except, of course, for his four younger friends who are now giggling. "What if you got a lot of stuff in your pants?" he asks. "Can you do a split?"

"It shouldn't matter what you have in your pants," you say. "You've got to practice, to stretch before you can get into a full split." Just as you decide you don't want anymore of this, a sixth boy shows up, littler than the last. He can't be a day over eight. His hair is cornrowed, and he wears a Denver Broncos T-shirt. He tells you his name is D'Andre.

"My name is also D'Andre," the young boy who had the erection offers. "We cousins. There a lot a D'Andres," he adds. You then find out that the ninth grader is named Mike, and the others are Chris, Ty and Keyan. The boys are now alternating between climbing the rope and making jumps for the trapeze. Mike can reach the bar with hardly a jump, and he hangs there for a moment struggling to do a chin-up. You ask if they have access to a jungle gym, and this starts them reminiscing about a time when they were being chased by dogs, but escaped by climbing some monkey bars.

"Smart," you say. "Dogs can't climb monkey bars. You can practice on them, you know." Older D'Andre can reach the trapeze bar with a good jump, but his chin-up is weak, and with a hurrumph, he lets go. Once again, you are concerned for their safety. This time you hop up on the trapeze to prevent them from playing with it.

"Do something," little D'Andre commands.

"Do that fast thing," Ty asks. Earlier, with gun in hand, he saw you doing mill circles—fast forward flips with legs scissoring around the bar. So now you launch into a series of moves. You beat to the bar and hold one leg forward in a split. You hook the forward leg and roll up in a one-leg monkey roll. You wrap an arm around the line, grip the bar, reach high for the line with the other arm and lift your legs from the bar in a move called the flag. Returning to the bar, you layback and ease into a banana, pull a foot to your head. You open into a split banana, hold the pose for a moment and then push your toes into the lines, your neck into the other end, balancing in a plank. You release from that position so that your spine rests on the bar, in a moon lady. From there you sit up and begin a furious series of mill circles, a trick that awes them all. You readjust to sitting on the bar for a moment before dropping into a fallen angel, nothing holding you but the flexion in your foot and the grip of your hand. They gasp as an audience should. You do love this thing. You are performing.

You flip to standing and do a high line series. You arabesque and then wrap your arms around the ropes and push them away from you as the bar lifts, a true testament of your strength. Unwrapping your arms, you flip upside down into a split, and then right side up with one leg stagged, a move called an arrow. The boys are quiet now. You flip back and plant one leg on the bar as you extend the other along the line into a split.

"That is tight," one boy cries out. You flip forward, smiling to yourself, happy that you still have it—the ability to wow a small crowd. You pop into a straddle balance, mainly to rest for a moment; you are upside down with your legs spread. You look out, nothing holding you but the arch in your back, the tension of your legs against the ropes, and when you look down, down below you, you see, sprawled on his back on the red and white mat, the tall boy—Mike—with his hand on his penis. The zipper of his baggy shorts is undone, and he's just lying there with his dick in his hand. You turn your head slightly and notice the older D'Andre, Chris, Keyan and Ty sitting on plastic chairs that line the brick wall, hands tucked under their shirts that hang loosely over their laps. Even little D'Andre is in on it. He stands with his hand on his crotch, giggling.

"Everybody out. Acrobatics is over," you yell as you move to an upright position on the bar; you cross your legs at the ankle. They scramble to get their shoes on and grab the two bikes they brought.

"I'm going to ejaculate," older D'Andre says as he crams his feet into his sneakers.

"Get out," you repeat because you feel repetition here is necessary, and get out they do. The boys leave the ARK. You see their blurred images through the window as they race along the street. You wonder if they'll return later to work on their bikes.

The children are gone, but you still sit up there on the trapeze, now resting against the line. You hear a voice. It's the stranger still talking to the dark-haired girl about her legal rights. You don't think of hopping down right away. Instead you stay up on the trapeze for a while, comfortable at that height.

Voices III.

MIKI ROHBOCK, JULIETTE KERNION,
SISTER MADELEINE HACHARD, WALT WHITMAN

MIKI ROHBOCK

Miki Rohbock runs her own tour company for Japanese travelers and is a coordinator of the Wonderful World Jazz Foundation Japan. She and her husband Steve rented a house in the Lakeview neighborhood of New Orleans before Katrina. They have temporarily resettled in a Chicago suburb with their five-year-old son. Miki's Japanese travel guide on New Orleans, slated for publication in October, has been postponed indefinitely.

We live in Elmhurst now, a suburb about thirty minutes away from downtown. It is largely a white, middle-class neighborhood. Coming from New Orleans, I feel like I'm in a foreign country. People here are so well-mannered, they cross the street where the white lines are … Elmhurst is a wonderful place, safe for children and has great schools. But when I think about my business, the community I belonged to, I just want to go home as quickly as I can.

I meet people from all walks of life through my work. Some come for the jazz, some for business. And I get to go and eat at places I wouldn't otherwise.

The Big Easy is rough around the edges and everybody works at their own pace. The Japanese are punctual and often want fast service. Some customers say, "I want this by tomorrow." But in New Orleans, you can only get a response a week later at best! Even for important events. And the Japanese love promises. We are in the middle of these two cultures.

My favorite spot in the city is the banks of the Mississippi River. The sunset looks different every day from there. I like watching the silhouettes of the city or chatting with friends who may be practicing the trumpet. Or eating beignets there.

Some of my best memories of New Orleans come from the way Japanese tourists have responded to the place. In the end, they always tell me, "We'll be back again!"

I had never cried in front of my child, but I did just once, a few days after we evacuated. My child comforted me, saying, "It's going to be okay. Tomorrow everything will be okay." We have lost a lot, but I've also learned a lot.

New Orleans has a deep history. Our spirit—everybody's spirit—hangs in the balance here, so I have confidence this place will be rebuilt and made even better. If New Orleans doesn't come back, neither will our spirits.

JULIETTE KERNION

Juliette Kernion frequented New Orleans' movie theaters while growing up outside the city. She now writes about film from her home in Austin, Texas.

The Robert E. Lee was our neighborhood babysitter for several years, even though we didn't live near the theater at all—we were smack in the middle of Metairie. The neighborhood moms would drive us to the theater every week for the Summer Movie Camp, drop us off for a couple of hours, and head for some shopping or lunch or whatever it was they did (heavy drinking, perhaps, considering some of the things we did at that age). It was a great deal for the price, as evidenced by the large audience with few adults. Summer day camps brought big groups of kids, too, accompanied by counselors who probably appreciated some quiet time in the dark.

The Robert E. Lee theater was the plushest-looking movie theater I ever saw as a child, and maybe even as a grownup. There was nothing to top it until I saw a play at the Saenger and fell in love with the ceiling of twinkling lights, but I didn't know until much later that it had ever been a movie theater. The Robert E. Lee was a single-screen theater with walls that were covered in what looked to me, at least when I was ten years old, like rich red velvet. I remember trying to find a time when no adults were looking so I could touch the walls and confirm that they were made of curtains. I didn't do it until we started going to summer kids' movies without adult supervision. Sure enough, it felt like velvet to me.

As the oldest neighborhood kid, I was in charge of the others, a job for which I received a couple of bucks each time, plus the movie and popcorn. Not a bad deal for me, but my brother and a couple of his rowdy little friends ensured that I earned every penny. On the other hand, what no one sees in the dark, doesn't happen. The movies were "family classics"—*Old Yeller*, the *Witch Mountain* films, *Yellow Submarine*. One week, the projectionist inadvertently showed the *Where the Red Fern Grows* reels out of sequence, which was perplexing but eventually sorted itself out.

Another week, someone made a programming error—did they think *Animal Crackers* sounded like a kids' title, did they confuse it with a Shirley Temple movie, or did someone actually believe that children would enjoy a feature-length Marx Brothers movie? Whatever the thinking (or lack thereof), it was a disaster. Twenty minutes into the film, the kids from day camps started leaving by the busload. The neighborhood kids were more patient than most but did eventually succumb to whining, running down the aisles and demanding that I call my mom to pick us up, the movie was soooo borrrrrring.

As a film geek, I wish I could say that I adored *Animal Crackers* and wanted to stay until the end, but I have to be honest. The entertaining comedy bits and lively music numbers were separated by long, long stretches of dull, talky romantic scenes. (I saw the movie again a couple of months ago and still find it that way.) I called my mom and we left before the movie ended. I remember that afternoon as a turning point for the Summer Movie Camp—after that year, the theater seemed to dumb down the kids' movie programming significantly to the level of cheap babyish animated junk. I can't verify that; it was my perception as a twelve-year-old. Maybe I just got too old for the movie series. We stopped going to the Summer Movie Camp and our parents found other activities to occupy our time.

We saw most movies at Joy's Panorama in Metairie or Joy's Cinema City in Kenner, since they were cheapest and closest to the house. In high school, I saw lots of movies in the theater near Lakeside Shopping Center. You had to be careful not to confuse Lakeside Cinema, adjacent to the mall, with Lakeside Theater, a short distance away on Veterans Boulevard. One of the four screens at Lakeside Theater was especially cool since it had been converted from a church.

We also saw movies at the Do-Drive In on Metairie Road. I think it was cheaper and easier to take three kids to a drive-in than it was to go to an indoor theater, especially at night. We saw *Star Wars* and *Grease* at the Do-Drive In. *Grease* outraged my mother, who found it inappropriate for kids and couldn't believe other people had recommended it. After that night, she wouldn't let us go to a non-Disney movie without checking the Catholic-sanctioned ratings in the *Clarion Herald*. We could see only films with "General" and "Adults and Adolescents" ratings. (Turned out that *Grease* had earned a "Morally Offensive" rating.)

Once in a very great while, we would see a movie downtown, often on nights when my dad watched us while my mom hosted a women's group meeting or party. My parents were usually the ones to see grown-up movies downtown at the Prytania or the Downtown Joy—one of those theaters showed *Harold and Maude* every year, and my dad hated to miss it.

In high school, I saw most movies on dates. But I never could seem to persuade my dates to go with me to the one theater where I'd never been, that always showed different fare than the other screens in town: the Prytania. My best friend in high school saw all kinds of movies there: she raved over *Betty Blue* and had even seen Jean-Luc Godard's scandalous film (to us Catholic schoolgirls, anyway) *Hail Mary*. I didn't get to the Prytania until I was a student at LSU. We went to the brand-new Galleria theaters instead, since it was adjacent to a video arcade that the guys just loved.

Sena Mall was another single-screen theater, not far from the Robert E. Lee, but entirely unremarkable in appearance. The only unique aspect of Sena Mall was that it showed *The Rocky Horror Picture Show* on the weekend, which was a fun thing to see in high school if you wanted something to do at midnight. While at LSU, I met a bunch of people who dressed up as characters from the cult movie and performed the show live underneath the screen while the movie was playing. They outfitted me with a glittery top hat and jacket and a sequined tube top, and for a couple of months I would ride down from Baton Rouge to New Orleans on weekend nights and act crazy in front of an audience armed with rice and water guns. I don't even want to think about the night the tube top slipped and fell. After that, it was pinned to a spaghetti-strap camisole.

Eventually the *Rocky Horror* gang broke up, but some of us still drove to New Orleans on the weekends, a little earlier in the day, to see movies at the Prytania and maybe have dinner somewhere cheap and fun like Magnolia Grill. And drinks. And perhaps dancing if we felt brave enough.

The Prytania let us down in my senior year at LSU by showing nothing but *Cinema Paradiso* for the better part of a year, but finally redeemed itself in the spring with *Cyrano de Bergerac* and *Tie Me Up! Tie Me Down!*

The New Orleans-area movie theaters I loved so much started closing shortly after I moved to Austin in 1991. I don't say there was a connection. During Christmas break after my first semester at the University of Texas, I spent nearly all the money in my checking account on movie posters at a fundraising sale at the Prytania. I wanted to keep the theater open and I wanted the poster for *The Cook, The Thief, His Wife and Her Lover* (which still hangs in my living room today, much to my parents' dismay). No one was shocked that I spent my meager funds on posters, but my family was shocked that I drove to the Prytania accompanied only by my little sister. The Prytania finally closed … and opened … and closed … and opened. Sena Mall closed and became a wine shop. I suffered through *Mrs. Doubtfire* at the old Joy's Panorama on Airline, which was pretty much a mess at that point, and the next time I visited town, it was closed for good. The building is gone and all that's left is pavement now. The Galleria became offices.

All my childhood theaters are gone now. The Do-Drive In is a strip mall. Lakeside Theater? A Lowe's. Lakeside Cinemas? A Bed, Bath and Beyond. Joy's Cinema City? I have no idea; I only know it's gone.

Most of my family still lives in Metairie. They escaped the worst of Katrina—they got out of town ahead of time and most of their houses were okay, except for my grandparents' old house in Lakeview.

Everyone in the family had been reported as fine before I saw the photo of the old Robert E. Lee movie theater. The theater had been closed for years and I heard it had been transformed into a grocery store. But the old façade was still in front, with giant old-fashioned letters spelling out the theater's name, and at least ten feet under water. I thought I was all done crying for a while but no, that photo broke me down again.

These days, I occasionally entertain wild fantasies of moving to New Orleans, fixing up the old Robert E. Lee and reopening it as an arthouse theater, but that's not really feasible. Still, it keeps at least one of the old theaters alive for me.

SISTER MADELEINE HACHARD

Sister Hachard left France in 1727 to join a convent in New Orleans. Her letters to her father, translated by Etolia S. Basso, were published in the 1948 anthology The World From Jackson Square.

We eat meat, fish, wild peas and beans and many fruits and vegetables, such as bananas, which are the most excellent of all the fruits, watermelons, sweet potatoes, figs, pecans and a thousand other fruits of which I did not know.

We live on buffalo, deer, wild geese and turkeys, rabbits, chickens, ducks, pheasant, partridge, quail and other fowl and game. The rivers here are full of monstrous fish, especially flounders, which are excellent fish, and a number of others which I never knew in France. They use much coffee and chocolate here, and there is a wild grape, larger than the French grape, but it is never in a bunch—but served in a plate like plums. That which is cheap and most common is rice with milk, and hominy, which is made of Indian corn, pounded in a mortar then boiled with water and served with butter or gravy. The people of Louisiana find this very good.

𝔇𝔞𝔦𝔩𝔶 ℭ𝔯𝔢𝔰𝔠𝔢𝔫𝔱.

NEW ORLEANS, TUESDAY, APRIL 4, 1848.

VENDORS of OYSTERS in NEW ORLEANS; WALT WHITMAN—THERE IS IN ALL cities bordering nigh onto the sea, a certain species of fish ycleped oysters, very much desired by the dwellers in said cities, and very much sold by certain individuals, of rare peculiarities, called oystermen.

In this goodly city of New Orleans (albeit, not so very good either), there abounds a class of worthy citizens, named as above, and who exercise the office and administration of fishes of this nature, styled, as we have said, oysters. The daily duty of these individuals—free citizens of a remarkably free city—is to vend by retail the interior fleshy and somewhat savory substance of these shell-fish, as above alluded to. The outer crust, or envelope of these, being of a tough, unyielding and indigestible quality, is rejected and thrown aside as worthless, nothing being eaten by the children of men but the puffy contents thereof. To sell such, is the business and daily care of those called, in common language, oystermen—the French style them écaille.

Food Will Save Us.

DAR WOLNIK

THE CITY OF NEW ORLEANS is defined by three things: music, corruption and food. The music is nurtured in the souls of hundreds of local musicians who grow up wearing their tubas home and playing them at the bus stops rather than dragging music cases to waiting SUVs like other American kids. The corruption is ingrained in three-hundred-year-old French and Spanish training, with ex-governors sitting in federal prisons and elected officials stuffing cash into their pockets while a hidden video camera whirs. The citizens of the city know America shakes its head at the stories that come out of New Orleans. But they can take the occasional snicker about politics Southern style because their city's food heritage rivals that of any place in the world.

The New Orleans food culture is much more complex than most visitors ever see the first, second or third time they visit; so complex that we can argue endlessly about the best gumbo recipe, where yaka mein is still sold or whether the muffuletta can be served warm at all. Almost all of our festivals revolve around food, including the famously named Shrimp and Petroleum Festival. Our food is not about Cajun or Creole; it is about neighborhoods, families and farmland.

The French Market

Pre-Katrina, more than four-thousand shoppers came each week to the Crescent City Farmers Market to share the most vital community experience: the gathering and sharing of food. Okra, satsumas, mirliton, drum and muscadine are a few of the seasonal items that draw hundreds of people when they first appear for sale at the market each year.

The farmers and fishers come from parishes (Louisiana's name for counties) such as Plaquemines, St. Bernard, St. Tammany, Washington, St. John, St. Charles and many more. These vendors will commonly commute one-hundred miles three or four times a week for the privilege of standing before a table loaded with their vegetables.

Farmers and fishers from far-off parishes are the backbone of each market, but some of the vendors hail from the city of New Orleans itself. One urban farmer breaks into Italian arias when sales are good; another has a wheel of luck that allows his shoppers to gamble on how many pieces of okra they get for a buck. The rural farmers shake their heads at this behavior but still respect anybody willing to stand outside to sell what they grow, city people or not. A farmer is a farmer; no one understands them but each other. Except ...

The chefs. The chefs share the same crazy dream that the farmers do: to provide amazing food to people, make almost no profit most of the year and spend fifteen hours a day doing it. No wonder farmers grow animated and helpful when they see a familiar grizzled face sticking out of a white kitchen coat. They recognize shared dreams and talents.

At the market, chefs are rock stars. People stare and whisper when they pass; they sidle up to them to overhear their conversations and even dare to approach and discuss a dish that had been prepared the last time they went to the fabled restaurant, much like a teenage fan would recite lyrics to a bass player. Chefs take it good-naturedly, but really they are here to talk to the farmers and fishers.

Home-kitchen shoppers make up the last third of this trinity. Many of them rival famous chefs in their ability to cook a spectacular dish. In fact, the market recently started asking regular folk to do cooking demonstrations as well.

Each of those groups suffered in this tragedy. The storm brought high winds and some rain to most of our farmers, but the biggest loss was felt by the fishing and citrus communities. The parishes that the shrimp, oyster and citrus families live and work in were the first to feel the devastating winds and storm surge, and they suffered greatly for it. The shrimping boats that cost over $100,000 were lying on their sides, their homes were gone and families were spread all over the region instead of picking oranges for the first Saturday market in October.

All the farmers, fishers and small businesses that make up the Crescent City Farmers Market faced the same deafening silence afterwards; no one was left in the city to buy their products. Not one restaurant, grocery store or hotel was buying anything. The market staff spent the weeks after the storm frantically trying to reach vendors over the phone and emailing anyone associated with the market in hopes of hearing news of a farmer. A few farmers and fishers were "deputized" (brought on as consultants) by the Crescent City Farmers Market as a way to reconnect the community of market vendors and to help their fellow vendors through the tedious chore of filling out long insurance forms. Not that the paperwork seems worth it; insurance policies and most government help are not designed to help these small entrepreneurs, so the staff at the market devotes time to rounding up private help and raising money.

The chefs spent a month sitting in far-off cities hoping they would not be the victims of water damage, looters and fire. Most make their profits during the fall and winter; they knew they were starting two or three months behind. All convention business had been canceled until March, so the big, fat corporate visits would not be a way to climb back to profitability. Restaurant staffs were flung far and wide, maybe as far as the diners. The chefs started the work with a sigh and a scrub brush.

As for the people that crowd the stalls shopping for fresh produce and sharing a laugh with a favorite vendor, they are part of the walking wounded. Homes are gone, and rebuilding will be costly. Families are renting houses in suburbs and nearby states and going to strange schools for the next few months. Will they come back? Some have said they will not, some are already rebuilding and some will stay away until the lure of an oyster po' boy or the beginning of strawberry season calls them back.

Many long phone conversations also focused on the return of the markets, deciding if the markets should change as the city will change. Should they include non-food items for the first time, with shop owners and chefs actually selling products alongside the regular vendors? Or is it more comforting to return to the exact same market that everyone left on August twenty-seventh? Either way, the local economy model is crucial in these twenty-first century frontier days of New Orleans; federal help is appreciated, but the ecology of our economy must be the model that Jane Jacobs taught us all — a rain forest with every drop of water reused and every drop of sunlight benefiting all.

Two things are true: the markets will return, and they will be an important presence in the restoration of the city. The town-square atmosphere of our markets and their inclusiveness cement their future in a city that expects food to save its soul.

*

Home Cooking.
TONI MCGEE CAUSEY, C.W. CANNON,
SARAH K. INMAN, RAY SHEA, JULIETTE KERNION

THE ANNUAL TATER LAUNCH PARTY

Every year, we host an annual Tater Launch Party, where we gather everyone we can (whoever is sober enough after a big New Year's night out). Everyone brings food (we usually cook lots of things like brisket, smoked hams and Carl's specialty, a favorite of the entire crowd: shrimp and corn soup.) The crowd arrives around lunchtime and sometime during the afternoon they will all go outside to the backyard where they will put a potato into a PVC pipe gun and will—through various mechanical means, some hair-spray as propellant and a flint—ignite said tater and shoot it out of the gun.

Yes, we are all about class 'round here, let me tell you.

The first year started innocently enough, I suppose. Friends were visiting from D.C., and they'd never been to Louisiana. Since the wife was a reporter for *The Washington Post*, I wanted to minimize their perception of Southerners as hicks and so had planned a couple of minor events to showcase Louisiana and our culture. The very first night, though, Carl and my friends started riffing at the restaurant on potatoes and ways to serve them. They hadn't even been drinking, and somehow, launching taters at people in a drive-through was suggested, and as I watched helplessly, Carl was explaining about shooting taters from a tater gun. The wife said she'd never heard or seen such a thing, and Carl promised her that she'd get to shoot a tater before she left.

So much for not being hicks. I don't know what I was expecting.

The next day went well, and I thought everyone had forgotten about the tater gun. It was remotely possible. (To this day, I wonder how I ever believed that. I mean, I know my husband. There is no stopping him from a crazy idea.) When our family and a few friends came over for lunch on New Year's day, I was busy mingling when I realized … my family was missing. The next thing I knew, Carl and Luke and Jake had broken out the tater gun and were outside with my visiting friends.

They were all shooting taters.

We live in a nice neighborhood, people. And my family was outside, shooting taters over the neighbors' yards at first, until they realized that maybe that wasn't such a bright idea. I was fairly mortified until I looked out there and realized the wife was aiming the tater gun and was so excited about shooting it, she was jumping with glee.

That's how The Annual Tater Launch began. Everyone leaving there that day said, "See you next year for the next tater launch" and the tradition was born. Each year the party grows. It's a wonderful mix of people, and I can't imagine a New Year's without it. We have lots and lots of food, a spacewalk for the little kids, and there are TVs everywhere showing whatever big game is on. Meanwhile, everyone eats an insane amount of food and shoots taters (now we build a big target so we don't litter the neighbors' yards), and general silliness prevails.

There has been only one emergency room visit. I am strangely proud of that.

— TONI McGEE CAUSEY

Carl Causey's Shrimp and Corn Soup (chowder)

1	stick butter
2	bunches green onions, coarsely chopped
1	bunch celery, finely chopped
3 *or* 4	carrots, grated
4	cans whole corn
3	cans cream corn
3	cans shrimp
2	cans crabmeat
1	can crab claw meat
3	cans cream of celery soup
1	quart half-and-half milk
$^1/_2$	gallon whole milk (*do not use skim or reduced fat milk*)
2	tablespoons Italian seasoning
2	capfuls Zatarain's liquid crab boil
	olive oil
	salt and pepper to taste (*Carl prefers freshly ground black pepper*)

You'll need a large sauce pot, capable of holding about three gallons of soup, and a skillet (large) for sautéing.

In the skillet, place four tablespoons of the olive oil and the coarsely chopped green onions. Drain water from all the cans of meat and then add to skillet. Turn heat onto medium, add the two capfuls of Zatarain's liquid crab boil. Add half stick of butter. Salt and pepper to taste. Sauté until the liquid has dissipated from the mixture. (The shrimp and crabmeat will contain water that will leech out of them when heat is applied.) When the water is mostly dissipated, add a half to a whole stick of butter, the chopped celery and continue sautéing until everything is tender or "loosened." Turn off heat.

Now, in the sauce pot, pour in the corn, cream of corn, the cream of celery soup, the quart of half-and-half, and add the contents of the skillet. Stir everything well. Add the milk—this will determine the consistency of the soup. Carl doesn't use quite all of the half-gallon of milk—he uses about three-quarters of that half-gallon. (I'm not sure what that measurement is.) Add the Italian seasoning and cook until the entire contents are a consistent temperature. Finally add the grated carrots and cook on medium-low until the carrots are very tender (which could take an hour or two). Check during cooking time for any need for additional salt or pepper.

Ready to serve. Will serve a large crowd. Best with hot French bread for dipping.

— TONI McGEE CAUSEY

Laura's Red Beans

My Louisiana vernacular cuisine stylings faced a major challenge in 2000, when I married a Jewish girl. Many New Orleanian Jews freely ignore the Torah's famous dietary restrictions, but not my wife—no shrimp po' boys, no oysters and no pork seasoning, which poses a major problem for the vast majority of vernacular Southern dishes. How to approximate the seemingly irreplaceable salt-essence of the liberally butchered Southland hog? My mom used to make what she called "Texas Red Beans," seasoned with stew beef, but while it tastes great, it tastes too different, too Texas. After many trials, I found the kosher-style approach with the closest taste to old style hamhock, salt-pork or pig-tail-stewed mama-made red beans and rice. The secret is a combo of chicken broth and turkey tasso (Richard's and Savoie's both make it) or, if you can't find that, a smoked turkey leg or neck. The kitchen should be floored in linoleum. If linoleum isn't available, just play the right music and knock on wood a lot. Should be served on Mondays or for any big party or event where you want a big pot of something.

1 pound red beans
1 medium white onion
1 medium bell pepper
2 long stalks celery
1 clove garlic (*or however much you want*)
½ lb. turkey tasso (*or 1 medium smoked turkey leg*)
6 cups chicken broth
1 tablespoon parsley
3 large bay leaves
½ teaspoon each white, red, black pepper
1 teaspoon paprika
salt, your call (*Southerners, Louisiana included, use at least double the amount other folks do*)
1 teaspoon olive oil
1 ½ *or* 2 cups Louisiana rice

Soak beans overnight or at least for a couple of hours. Drain and add to chicken broth. Bring to a boil, adding however much water you need to keep liquid about a half-inch over the beans, allowing the mixture to thicken without becoming thick enough to stick. Add finely chopped onion, bell pepper, celery, garlic and coarsely chopped tasso (or just toss the bird leg in there). Add herbs and olive oil (the oil protects from sticking and contributes to the creamy texture). After mixture comes to a rolling boil, reduce heat and simmer, covered, for three hours. Stir and taste frequently. Start drinking your beer or wine during the tasting process so you can get a sense of what your guests will taste when dining. After about two or two-and-a-half hours of cooking, take a flat spoon and smash some of the beans along the side of the pot—this is what gives Creole-style red beans the distinctive creamy texture. Serve with plain boiled Louisiana white rice, French bread (baguette) and butter, and a bottle of Tabasco or other Louisiana hot sauce on the table.

— C.W. CANNON

Saint Patrick's Day Parade Cabbage Soup

Vow not to go to this year's Saint Patrick's Day parade, but get dragged out to Magazine Street anyway. It's a nice day, you reason, as you're handed a beer. Keep your head up, watching for flying cabbages, the ones being tossed from the floats. Make sure to snatch one, just one cabbage, a small, young, tightly packed cabbage. Take it home with all the other parade junk beads and moon pies—and prepare to make cabbage soup like the good Polish girl you are.

Peel away the first layer of leaves and then slice up or shred the cabbage. If you've had too much to drink, hand over the knife to someone else. While you're at it with the knife, dice up a small onion and a few cloves of garlic. Chop up a few carrots and some mushrooms, maybe a potato, whatever vegetables you've got lying around that seem like they might go well in cabbage soup.

In a large pot, fry the onions and garlic in a little vegetable oil. Then add about five cups of chicken broth. Cover the pot and bring the liquid to a boil. Once the water's boiling, add the diced cabbage and carrots and other vegetables. Add more water or broth, depending on how you like your veggie-to-liquid ratio. Simmer for about twenty minutes, stirring occasionally.

Now for a little flavor. Add a pound of your favorite pork—kielbasa, hamhocks or bacon. Shake in some pepper; you probably have no need for extra salt. Sprinkle in some caraway seeds. Open a small can of sauerkraut and add that to the mix. Stir up the contents of the pot, again adding liquid if it seems necessary. Cover the pot again and simmer for an hour or however long you need to nap away the afternoon's revelry.

— SARAH K. INMAN

Crawfish Fortuna Omelettes

This isn't really a traditional family recipe or anything, but it's something that's evolved over the years. The sauce is actually based on one by Alex Patout, from his great and sadly out-of-print book, *Cajun Home Cooking.*

When my wife and I lived in San Francisco, there was this little breakfast joint down the block from our house, on the corner of Haight and Belvedere, called Fortuna's. Their Mommy Fortuna Omelette was our favorite hangover cure, but when the place suddenly closed down, we thought the recipe was gone forever.

A few years later we'd moved to Austin and I'd cooked Patout's Shrimp Ms. Ann for some guests. We had a bunch of the sauce left over so I froze some of it. Several weeks later I was making spinach omelettes and, on a whim, I thawed out a little of the sauce and added it to the recipe, and after the first bite, my wife and I looked at each other and exclaimed, "Holy #$@%! Mommy Fortuna Omelettes!"

Later we added the crawfish. We like crawfish.

Measurements are kind of approximate. I don't really measure much.

- 1   stick butter
    dry vermouth
    juice of 2 lemons
- ⅛ cup Worcestershire sauce
- ½ cup chopped green onions
- ½ cup chopped parsley
    cayenne pepper
    salt
- 3 cloves garlic, finely chopped
- ½ pound Louisiana crawfish tails
    eggs
    grated Monterey Jack cheese
    fresh spinach
    sour cream

Blanch the spinach until it wilts a little. Melt the butter in a skillet over medium high heat, then add the garlic, a splash of dry vermouth, lemon juice, Worcestershire sauce, a pinch of cayenne, pinch of salt and the parsley and green onions. Let cook for three minutes, then add the crawfish tails and coat well with the sauce. Cook for another minute or two and then lower the heat to keep warm.

Make omelettes the way you usually make cheese omelettes. Add a little grated cheese, then lay on a little spinach, spoon in a generous helping of crawfish tails and some of the sauce, then a smattering of more cheese to hold it together.

Fold the omelette and plate it. Garnish with a dollop of sour cream, a sprig of parsley and an orange slice, and serve with curly fries. Yes, curly fries.

— RAY SHEA

Oyster Dressing

I've had some yummy Thanksgiving dinners in all kinds of places, but it doesn't quite feel like Thanksgiving without oyster dressing. In the Yankee frozen tundra, they make "stuffing" out of bread cubes to accompany turkey, but it's called "dressing" in the South. I was grown-up before I ate stuffing that someone had actually stuffed into a turkey and cooked, which freaked me out. My family usually serves two kinds of dressing: my mom's cornbread dressing, which is fabulous, and oyster dressing as in the recipe below. The chopped oysters help make the dressing much less dry than other types of dressing or stuffing without having to stick anything in a bird's rear end.

- 1 pound pork sausage
- 2 large loaves stale French bread
- 2 onions, chopped
- 1 teaspoon thyme
- 2 bell peppers, chopped
- 2 bay leaves
- 6 ribs celery, chopped
- 6 dozen oysters (*reserve water*)
- 4 cloves garlic, chopped
  salt and pepper to taste
- 1 bunch parsley, chopped
  Italian style bread crumbs
- 1 ½ stick butter

Fry sausage until well cooked and drain several times on paper towels. Set aside. Sauté chopped onions, bell pepper, celery, garlic, parsley and green onions in butter until cooked down. Break up stale French bread and put in a pot of water until it is saturated. Squeeze out the bread to dry. Add to the seasoning with the cooked sausage. Add the thyme and bay leaves. Cook about twenty minutes, stirring to make sure it does not stick to the bottom of the pan. Drain the oysters (reserving the water) and chop them into small pieces. Add the oysters to the pot and some of the oyster water if the dressing seems dry. Cook an additional ten minutes, stirring occasionally. Put dressing in a large three-quart greased casserole and top with Italian-style bread crumbs. Bake at 350 degrees for thirty to forty minutes.

— JULIETTE KERNION

Oyster Patties

Oyster patties are a big part of my family's Christmas celebrations. Every year, NaNa (my dad's mom) would make them as appetizers before big holiday dinners. Now that she's gone, my mom tries to remember to find oysters and make the patties on Christmas Eve. I didn't like oysters when I was growing up, but I liked oyster patties, maybe because the oysters are all chopped up. NaNa would usually buy the patties in two sizes: the little cocktail ones that kids could handle easily and the big ones that were practically a meal. The pastry shells always came from McKenzie's Bakery, which is closed now, so I don't have any idea where you can buy them these days. (I also don't know what they're called outside New Orleans—we always called them "oyster patty shells.")

12	large patties or 36-48 cocktail patties (*oval pastry shells*)
2	sticks butter
1	cup green onions, chopped fine (*include greens*)
2	cups minced celery
2	well-rounded cooking spoons flour
3-4	dozen oysters, chopped in small pieces
1	cup oyster water
3	cups milk
1/4	cup parsley
1	teaspoon thyme
1	teaspoon salt and pepper
2	dashes Tabasco

Melt butter on low heat. Do not brown. Mix in celery and green onions. When celery is limp, add flour, stirring until smooth. Stir in oysters and salt, pepper, Tabasco and parsley. Reduce heat to simmer and allow a few minutes before stirring in milk. When milk is added, watch closely to prevent mixture from bubbling, as milk will curdle. Let simmer until mixture is thick. Test with spoon; when it drips slowly from spoon, remove from fire. Let cool and fill patties. Place on a cookie sheet in 350-degree preheated oven for fifteen to twenty minutes or until patties are crisp. Be careful when serving them straight out of the oven—the patty filling can get molten-hot.

—JULIETTE KERNION

*

Voices IV.

MARK TWAIN

The great American writer penned the following description of New Orleans as viewed from a riverboat in his 1883 book, Life on the Mississippi.

The approaches to New Orleans were familiar; general aspects were unchanged. When one goes flying through London along a railway propped in the air on tall arches, he may inspect miles of upper bedrooms through the open windows, but the lower half of the houses is under his level and out of sight. Similarly, in high-river stage, in the New Orleans region, the water is up to the top of the inclosing levee-rim, the flat country behind it lies low—representing the bottom of a dish—and as the boat swims along, high on the flood, one looks down upon the houses and into the upper windows. There is nothing but that frail breastwork of earth between the people and destruction.

THE GARBAGE INDEX

One way New Orleanians gauge the size of the Mardi Gras crowds is by looking at the garbage they produce. Of course, it's an inexact science that also includes hotel occupancy rates, airline flights and other key indicators, like total arrests. Here's a look at the garbage totals and crowd estimates for Mardi Gras around the turn of the century.

YEAR	GARBAGE (IN TONS)	CROWDS
1997	946	1.5 million
1998	800	1.8 million
1999	932	2.0 million
2000	1,230	2.0 million+
2001	1,520	2.0 million

Source: *The Times-Picayune*

CHARLES LYELL

Lyell was a British lawyer and geologist who lived from 1797 to 1875. He was a friend and contemporary of Charles Darwin. Lyell wrote two popular books in the 1840s detailing his travels across the United States. This passage was taken from the second book, A Second Visit to the US, *published in 1849.*

Feb. 23 (1846).—We arrived here in New Orleans on the day before the Carnival. From the time we landed in New England to this hour, we seemed to have been in a country where all, whether rich or poor, were labouring from morning till night, without ever indulging in a holiday. I had sometimes thought that the national motto should be, "All work and no play." It was quite a novelty and a refreshing sight to see a whole population giving up their minds for a short season to amusement. There was a grand procession parading the streets, almost everyone dressed in the most grotesque attire, troops of them on horseback, some in open carriages, with bands of music, and in a variety of costumes—some as Indians, with feathers in their heads, and one, a jolly fat man, as Mardi Gras himself. All wore masks, and here and there in the crowd, or stationed in a balcony above, we saw persons armed with bags of flour, which they showered down copiously on anyone who seemed particularly proud of his attire. The strangeness of the scene was not a little heightened by the blending of Negroes, quadroons and mulattoes in the crowd; and we were amused by observing the ludicrous surprise, mixed with contempt, of several unmasked, stiff, grave Anglo-Americans from the north, who were witnessing for the first time what seemed to them so much mummery and tomfoolery. One wagoner, coming out of a cross-street, in his working-dress, drove his team of horses and vehicle heavily laden with cotton bales right through the procession, causing a long interruption. The crowd seemed determined to allow nothing to disturb their good humour; but although many of the wealthy Protestant citizens take part in the ceremony, this rude intrusion struck me as a kind of foreshadowing of coming events, emblematic of the violent shock which the invasion of the Anglo-Americans is about to give to the old régime of Louisiana. A gentleman told me that, being last year in Rome, he has not seen so many masks at the Carnival there; and, in spite of the increase of Protestants, he thought there had been quite as much "flour and fun" this year as usual. The proportion, however, of strict Romanists is not so great as formerly, and tomorrow, they say, when Lent begins, there will be an end of the trade in masks; yet the butchers will sell nearly as much meat as ever. During the Carnival, the greater part of the French population keep open house, especially in the country.

FAT TUESDAY

Carnival Season officially begins on January 6, which is Twelfth Night, or the end of Christmas Season. The season ends on Fat Tuesday, or Mardi Gras, a day that can fall anywhere from February 3 to March 9. Mardi Gras ends with the police, on foot and on horseback, moving down Bourbon Street to clear out the crowds at midnight. The police are immediately followed by street sweepers and garbage trucks. All the precious beads that are left in the street are quickly mingled with muck and garbage and hauled away. Future Fat Tuesdays will fall on the dates below.

2006	February 28	2014	March 4
2007	February 20	2015	February 17
2008	February 5	2016	February 9
2009	February 24	2017	February 28
2010	February 16	2018	February 13
2011	March 8	2019	March 5
2012	February 21	2020	February 25
2013	February 12		

I Was a Teenage Float Grunt.

RAY SHEA

THE MARDI GRAS FLOATS LEAVE PUDDLES. Puddles which should be avoided, if you know what's good for you. You'd like to think maybe somebody just spilled their beer, but let me tell you.

When I was a kid, one of the highlights of the Carnival season was getting to work in the parades.

The krewes all used Boy Scout volunteers to operate the moving parts on the floats—make the animated heads spin, make the dragons go up and down, that sort of thing. For six hours of grubby, tedious work in cramped conditions, we got paid fifteen bucks and got to cart off enough beads and doubloons to fill a couple Schwegmann's bags. We thought we were the luckiest guys on earth.

Our first day of float work, we arrived in the chilly, gray late afternoon at the staging area of the parade and got our float assignments. Much to my surprise, my very first gig as a float grunt had me rubbing elbows with celebrities. Usually the older boys got the prestigious floats, but for some reason some other new kid and I were assigned to the riverboat float that carried Doc Severinsen and another celebrity. Our job was to sit inside and turn a crank to make the paddle wheels turn. OK, so we weren't going to actually see the Doc, much less interact with him, but we'd be on the same float with him. Us and sixty other guys.

A guy from Blaine Kern, the float manufacturer, helped us up the ladder onto the float, which was still deserted. He showed us the little door to the inside, where the paddle wheel controls were located. Right next to the pee bucket. Super.

We spent a little time trying to figure out how to get the wheels to turn, but the dang things wouldn't budge. A little investigation revealed the problem; the riders had already loaded their boxes of throws on board, and since it was such a tight fit, they'd crammed boxes of beads and doubloons and cups into every nook and cranny—into, under and around the base of the paddle wheel. There was no way this thing was going to turn without a major reorganization, so once the riders climbed aboard (some needing much help, since they were well-lubricated in advance of the formal festivities), we approached one.

"Excuse me, sir?"

"Hey, podna, what's up? You want a beer?"

I was fourteen. It wouldn't be legal for me to have a beer in New Orleans for at least a few more months. Besides, we were under strict orders from the Scout leaders: anybody caught drinking wouldn't be allowed on any more parades for the rest of the season.

"Uh, no thank you. We're Boy Scouts, we're supposed to make the paddle wheel turn during the parade, but it's jammed with all these boxes."

The guy looked at the boxes, tried the wheel himself and decided to check with the float captain. The float captain tried the wheel and then sagely announced that they'd rather have the extra room to store throws than have a functioning paddle wheel. The throws were the important thing, after all. So my friend and I were relegated to sitting inside the float next to the piss bucket doing nothing for the rest of the night. The most important rule, we had been told by the Scout leaders, was that we must stay out of sight during the parade because we weren't masked. (The second most important rule was the "no beer" thing.)

Just before we got under way, they fired up the generator that powers the thousands of lights that illuminate the float as it rolls down Canal Street, and we realized that our little hideaway inside was really a gas chamber where we'd soon die of carbon-monoxide poisoning. So we checked with our float guy again, and he checked with the captain again.

"Yeah, you don't want to sit in there all night, it's not safe. Besides, it stinks like piss in there. You boys can just sit out here next to the paddle wheel and stay out of sight."

"OK, thanks."

"No problem. You boys want a beer?"

"No, sir, we're not allowed."

"Awright."

So there we were. Freezing cold, damp, sitting on the floor in the spilled beer with no room to stretch our legs, while the crowd screamed "Hey mista! Hey mista! Throw me somethin' mista!" and the riders heaved bag after bag of throws over the side and every once in a while almost heaved themselves over the side to get close to some girl on her boyfriend's shoulders. We were the only two kids in the whole city who were at the parade and not having fun.

And then, the float captain delivered us from our misery.

"Y'all looking for something to do? Doc's hands are too cold to unwrap beads fast enough to throw them, so maybe you could go up there and help him out."

We looked at each other, and I replied, "But we're not supposed to be where anybody can see us."

"You're supposed to be our Boy Scout helpers, right? You go up there and just stay low and if you get in any trouble you tell them I said it's OK."

Reassured, we made our way up the tiny stairs to the very tippy-top front of this mighty paddle wheel float and started unwrapping beads for Doc and for the other celebrity up there, some old lounge singer whom I'd never heard of. We'd hand them up as fast as they could throw them—beads, doubloons, anything—and every once in a while Doc would see a pretty girl and say, "Oh, look at that! Give me some of those long beads, quick!" And he's laughing and cussing up a storm and having a ball, and we're looking at each other and laughing and thinking nobody is ever going to believe this.

During one of those lulls, when we'd been sitting still for a long time while some grand poobah krewe officer up ahead was probably toasting the mayor or some such, Doc turned to us and said, "I'm starving, did you fellas bring anything to eat?"

I dug around and found the bag lunch that my mom had packed for me.

"I have a ham sandwich."

"Oh, can I have a bite?" he asked, and the sandwich disappeared from my hand before I could protest and was devoured in seconds.

"That was good! Got anything else?"

"Uh … Fritos?"

Woof. Gone.

"All we need now is a couple of stiff drinks. Say, you fellas don't have anything to drink, do you?"

"No, we're not allowed."

"That's too bad."

And so it went, for mile after mile, until we rolled into the Riverwalk where the krewe's ball was in full swing. Compared to the late-night crowds on Canal Street, the Riverwalk folks were incongruous. Guys in tuxedos, girls in gowns, but completely schnockered and yelling for beads and doubloons, just like the hordes outside.

And in the Riverwalk, as the riders staggered, fell or were carried off the floats, our reward awaited. They all needed to unload their excess throws, and we were only too willing to take as much as they'd give us. The Lord had conferred His bounty upon us, made us rich beyond our wildest dreams, and it was only the first parade.

The next night, though, would not be such a cakewalk.

They actually expected us to do real work. And we would learn all about those mysterious puddles.

At the staging area up on Napoleon, early that next evening, the driver showed us how to duck under the front skirting of the float and climb up inside. The entire structure was a big wooden frame suspended over a trailer, with a plywood platform just barely big enough for the two of us to sit on. Two ropes controlled the big animated head on the float. One rope turned the head to the left, the other to the right. A small hole cut in the front wall gave us a way to see out a little bit and to yell to the driver if we needed him.

"Y'all 'll be all right up on that platform," he said. Then he warned, "Don't just climb down without telling me, though, 'cause if I start moving, ya like to get run over."

And with that, he ducked back under and out, and fired up the tractor.

The noise as the parade got under way was deafening. Tractors. Generators. Marching bands. And as we turned the corner from Napoleon onto St. Charles, the screaming crowds again. Unlike the previous parade, on this night we were right down at street level. Whenever the float stopped for an extended period, the crowds would press in, people screaming for beads, banging the side walls all around us.

After a while we figured out that the ropes were easier to control by one person at a time, as long as that person abandoned the platform and climbed out onto one of the framing beams, suspended directly over the pavement below like a kid hanging off a tree limb in his backyard. OSHA would have a cow over the whole situation: underage workers, unsafe working conditions, inebriated drivers …

Inebriated drivers?

As any Carnival-goer who is reasonably observant knows, a fair number of float drivers celebrate the season in style while on the job. You'll often see a can of beer nestled between the driver's legs as he navigates, and it's not unusual for kindly parade watchers all along the route to top him off when he's running low.

Our driver was no exception.

We were at a dead stop in absolutely massive crowds, somewhere in the vicinity of Lee Circle, when he popped up inside.

"Woooooo, crazy out there!" he exclaimed. "Gotta take a piss."

He set down his beer on our platform, unzipped and took a whiz right there in the street, secluded in the relative privacy of the float innards. The puddle spread and ran in rivulets across the pavement, under the float and out into the crowd.

Though we were Boy Scouts and had experience with all manner of scatological humor, camp pranks, fart jokes and the like, we were aghast. Nay, appalled even. Even though we knew we were going to drive off and leave the puddle behind in a few minutes, it was like he had come into our living room and peed on the floor.

"If y'all need to go, be sure to let me know so that I don't drive off while you're standing on the cee-ment. Y'all want a beer or anything?"

"No, thanks, we're not allowed."

"Awright," he shrugged and ducked back out.

We decided to decline the invitation to commit public urination, private as it was. I wasn't entirely sure that if we told him to stop for a few minutes so we could pee that he'd remember to wait, in his somewhat impaired state of mind. And if getting run over by a float was not high on my list of spectacular ways to die, doing it with my fly open seemed even less glorious.

We would make it to the Riverwalk without further drama. We would claim our Schwegmann's bags full of throws. And we would have a nice, quiet, private pee. And then we'd head home to Algiers and leave the backstage lunacy of Carnival behind for another year.

Every year Mardi Gras produces thousands of new stories and new memories, most of them pretty funny. Every New

Orleanian has an anecdote about how many beads they caught the year they yelled "Uncle Jawn!" at every float that went by, or the first time they showed Grandpa Tony from back East how to step on a doubloon first before bending over to pick it up, or the first time their own kids were big enough to watch the parades sitting up in the ladder seat that Papa made for them, or the year they had to sneak across the river to the French Quarter without telling their parents because the police went on strike during Mardi Gras and Mom was afraid the National Guard would start shooting if the crowds got crazy.

But for me, my favorite personal story will always be about the year that my mom got to feed Doc Severinsen and I learned how floats pee.

*

The New Orleans Manifesto.

C.W. CANNON

This manifesto was handed out in leaflet form by costumed revelers during the 2003 Mardi Gras.

In this time of rapid change, of dreams of "progress," of the widespread desire of many of our people to be "regular Americans," let us remind ourselves not to lose the most precious aspects of our more localized identity. Our neighborhoods are the Creole Districts—the French Quarter, Treme, St. John, Marigny and Bywater. Through peculiar circumstances, we have evolved a unique kind of society. Architect Robert Cangelosi has reminded us that the reason our housing is so lovely is "preservation by neglect." Indeed, economic underdevelopment is probably the reason our culture and way of life remain distinct as well. As we look forward hopefully to greater economic opportunity, let us seek to preserve, or to salvage, those social features which also make us beautiful. Let us consider the following four principles as fundamental, as those aspects of our different little world that we wish to preserve for our posterity and for the benefit of all people in the world:

I. PUBLIC HABITATION OF THE PUBLIC SPACE

They say New Orleans is a great place to be poor. Why? Housing costs are still relatively cheap, as are other cost-of-living indices. On the other hand, government-sponsored social services are also comparatively few and poorly administered. But in a city where a third of the population lives below the poverty line, a culture of free and collective amusement has emerged. New Orleanians entertain themselves in the street, often to the chagrin of hapless drivers. It continues to be legal (unlike anywhere else in America) to consume alcoholic beverages on the public ways. The French Quarter is an open-air free family fun park, with live music, magicians, jugglers, mimes and outrageous freelance paraders. Elsewhere in the Creole Districts, on Sundays, the s.o.p. American drive from church to TV football is interrupted by funky marching bands followed by Second Line dancers for blocks, under clouds of marijuana smoke—all with a police escort! Today, of course, Giuliani-ism, a northern import, is driving elected officials to "clean up" the French Quarter. The problem is, homeless folks, including our iconic "winos," are an age-old thread in the fabric of French Quarter life. When I was a kid, the Quarter was much more shabby, smelly and stocked with implacable, unmoneyed eccentrics than it is today. Authorities have lately been cracking down on street musicians, tarot readers and, yes, bums (whether the old dark-suited variety or the new gutter-punk type) to make the Quarter more amenable, not so much to tourists—whose whole attraction to New Orleans is wild-side flirtation anyway—but to the new condo locusts from Dallas, Florida and the plain places beyond. They need to realize that our culture of unauthorized public performance is just as indispensable to our identity as cuisine and architecture. The easy interaction of New Orleanians of all walks of life at streetcar and bus stops, grocery stores, etc., is predicated on all of us feeling "at home" in the public space. The way Second Lines seize control of ugly highway underpasses and elevate them to Utopias of Funk, the dancers on people's cars and on storefront awnings, it's all a symbolic act of occupation of the public space at a time when the rest of America advances toward the total privatization of everything.

II. ANTI-PURITANISM

Let us thank the gods for the generous strains of French, Spanish and, above all, African cultures that have inoculated New Orleans against the body-hating, life-hating Puritanism that brutally curtails the sensual lives of too many Americans. Praise Bacchus, praise Legba. New Orleanians insist on their right to party and recognize that the party-drive is not a frivolous one. The Creole Districts of New Orleans have been historic centers of sexual freedom. That's why we can boast one of the oldest, outest gay scenes in the country, including America's oldest continuously open gay bar. Many Gay Americans today are ready to downplay their sexuality in order to stress the commonality they share with other Americans in the many nonsexual aspects of life. They might be surprised to note that the Gay Pride celebrations so dear to gays around the country get comparatively little play in New Orleans. The New Orleans LGBT community saves its energy for the Southern Decadence Festival, a Homo-Con free zone where gay sexuality is openly practiced, performed—in the street—in a way that would be impossible in any other city. But it's not only gays who are allowed to have a sexuality in New Orleans; straight people are invited to party too! When I was but a wee boy, I witnessed man-on-man action by ecstatic exhibitionists in the public space, but I was able to check out boy-girl play, too. The public display of nudity and sexuality is liberating, an act of revolt against the puritan witch-hangers that want us to lead lives of private, self-loathing shame.

Besides sex, of course, there's intoxication, and that other realm of Bacchus, masking. We're proud that New Orleans continues to have the most liberal alcohol laws in the nation—24/7, anywhere. Let me quote the slogan of the Mystick Krewe of T.O.K.I.N.: "New Orleans: Proud to Crawl Home." We're proud that we, and only we, host the mother of all parties: Mardi Gras, where literally a million people mask and get wasted, without shame, in the beautiful streets of our Cool Mom city. But we can do better. The one city in the world that New Orleans should look to as a role model is Amsterdam: let's legalize it, y'all. Let the feds come after us; they've never liked us, anyway. They forced us to shut down Storyville (our red-light district), forced us to raise the legal drinking age to twenty-one (we were the last state to give in). But guess what? They still think we're degenerates.

III. KEEP IT "SLOW-BREWED"

Mardi Gras, Second Lines blocking traffic—isn't this stuff bad for business? Well, yes. Also bad for business is the near Communist pace of service in government offices as well as private commercial establishments. Tell your friends from out of town it's "French-style" service. Nobody seems to be in a rush. Many outsiders pull their hair out over our fabled inefficiency. Clearly the school board and other public agencies should try to pick up the pace and get their act together, but what about rank-and-file citizens? Is the slow pace really that bad for us? Or is it in fact good, a more healthful alternative to the drive-like-hell and live-for-your-boss attitude that so many Americans seem to think is a sane way of life? There was a great deal of local resistance to the placement of a Wal-Mart in the Garden District. Supporters pointed out how convenient it would be to park in the giant lot and pick up your roofing tiles and your lettuce at the same location. But barely hanging on in the Creole Districts is the residue of a former way of life: the bakery, the farmer's market, the hardware store, the drugstore—all in different buildings! It takes a long time to trudge to all these different places. And there's no point in driving because there's never a place to park; many of these little places don't have parking lots. You have to ride your bike or walk. Fast food's hard to come by, too. Apparently most New Orleanians would rather get a po' boy or a plate lunch than a Big Mac, because we have so few national fast-food chains. This means we end up spending more time getting lunch than the go-getters in Houston. Many folks complained about the resurrected streetcar lines because the bus gets downtown much faster. But we want pretty, not fast. And that's OK. We need to convert the slow pace of our daily routines—our eating, transportation practices, pointless street conversation with strangers—from a perceived weakness into ideology. Instead of New Orleans speeding up to "catch up" with America, here's a radical idea: maybe America oughtta slow down and notice the texture of living, what it feels like to walk, for example. Relax baby, have a beer. Take care of that chore tomorrow. The boss can wait. Marx called for a five-hour work day, and that should be the goal. The sad fact today about the work scene in America, and in the "Global Economy" (shudder), is not so much that lazy capitalists don't work, but that workaholics expect everybody to live the insane, destructive way they do. That "work-ethic" thing is a Puritan pickpocket. Don't believe it.

IV. MISCEGENATION FOREVER

Ask any random tourist (above the frat-boy level) what's special about New Orleans and you'll hear about the Holy Trinity of New Orleans travel marketing: food, music, architecture. They're not wrong, either. But what we need always to remember is that all of these institutions, as well as the attributes I've touched on above, are the products of miscegenation. The term "miscegenation," like "queer," and like the "n" word, started off its career as a derogative. Puritanical Confederate types were scared to death during Reconstruction that black people and white people might start shacking up and making brave new babies that would overturn their evil world. In fact, that did happen, especially in the Creole Districts, where, even before the Civil War, open "cohabitation" was afoot. A cursory glance at the multifarious hues on New Orleanian faces is testament to those heroic ances-tors who did what the hell they wanted despite the threats and punishments of the monsters in power. I'm not pretending that many interracial liaisons were not exploitative, but I am asserting that not all were. I've heard too much oral history from my own people, and from other New Orleanians, to believe that all interracial sex was coerced. Remember, Puritans, even the pseudo-feminists among them, would have us believe that sex is "degrading," therefore *always* coerced. Anyway, miscegenation, which we believe to be beautiful and good, need not involve actual fucking. It stands as a cultural paradigm, indeed, as an axiom for measuring a special quality in all New World artifacts and social practices: the "quality" of an American work of art is to be judged by the degree of its miscegenation. Also, in this day and age, miscegenation need not be limited to black-white mixing. When I get lunch at my neighborhood po' boy and seafood joint, the Vietnamese proprietors serve me up Creole blue collar Asian Fusion. This fruitful, playful mixing-it-up, designated by the paradigm of miscegenation, need not be limited to racial categories, either. That's why I, a "straight" male, can have a high time with the gay men at the Southern Decadence Festival. At any rate, bi is the orientation most privileged by proud miscegenationists. Bi polygamy, to be exact. How odd that New Orleans, so peripheral among American cities, should supply most elegantly the model for appreciating American culture writ large! It's because the Creole Districts were multicultural before multicultural was cool, to wit, way before the birth of that blond sweetheart, American Pie. Let us end with a shout: miscegenation yesterday, miscegenation today, miscegenation forever!

We hold these truths not only to be self-evident, but self-propagating. Everyone in the world who is feeling these basic principles is a New Orleanian. Every New Orleanian who is *not* feeling these principles is also a New Orleanian because the gods adore difference and abhor sameness. See y'all in the streets. *Laissez les bon temps rouler.*

LAGNIAPPE

We picked up one excellent word—a word worth traveling to New Orleans to get; a nice limber, expressive, handy word—"lagniappe." They pronounce it lanny-yap. It is Spanish—so they said. We discovered it at the head of a column of odds and ends in the Picayune, *the first day; heard twenty people use it the second; inquired what it meant the third; adopted it and got facility in swinging it the fourth. It has a restricted meaning, but I think the people spread it out a little when they choose. It is the equivalent of the thirteenth roll in a "baker's dozen." It is something thrown in, gratis, for good measure. The custom originated in the Spanish quarter of the city ... If the waiter in the restaurant stumbles and spills a gill of coffee down the back of your neck, he says, "For lagniappe, sah," and gets you another cup without extra charge.*

— MARK TWAIN, from *Life on the Mississippi*

*

Professor Stevens Goes to Mardi Gras.

REX NOONE

PROFESSOR STEVENS HAD BEEN TEACHING philosophy at the University of New Orleans for over twenty years. This year he decided that he should see Mardi Gras in the French Quarter, on Bourbon Street. He had heard about Bourbon Street. He would not go there as a participant, not as one of the mob. He would go to observe, to study the culture; he would go as a sociologist, as an anthropologist.

During previous Mardi Gras weekends he had stocked up on food, water and books and remained inside of his Mid-City house the entire time, Friday through Tuesday. On those weekends, he would seclude himself in scholarship: not a thought ever made it out to the street. This year was different. Call it a whim; call it a long neglected thought that had finally earned some attention. Whatever the reason, Professor Stevens set off for the bus stop.

He had nice posture, a small tweed cap and a compact round belly. At the end of the day, he would have only one of these.

When he stepped off of the bus, the air seemed to be filled with the sound of laughter. People were breathing that laughter, tossing it back and forth all over Royal Street. Random laughter of this kind made Professor Stevens uncomfortable, ever since elementary school.

Ignoring that distraction as much as he could, he walked through the French Quarter, observing. He observed the Pope shaking hands with Elvis Presley, having their picture taken together. Neither was quite authentic. He observed the Cowardly Lion slumped in a doorway, holding a large bottle of alcohol, half-empty. The fake mane looked more alive than the man. This was mid-afternoon, and it seemed that the party had started long ago. He observed a woman wearing a burka, completely covered from head to waist, where sexy fishnet stockings began, working their way down to some shiny high heels.

The urge to mask oneself both physically and psychologically, noted Professor Stevens. *To transform oneself in a way that alters the social code, allowing such primal callings as sex and intoxication — two means for obliterating the self — to dominate for a day. Only to have those codes reinforced in the morning, when one awakes as a hungover secretary or a debauched bank teller.*

"Nice hat, dude," said a shirtless man carrying a surfboard in one hand and holding the other up for a high five.

Professor Stevens stepped to the side, to avoid that hand. This was Mardi Gras: no comment about a cap could be considered insulting. But Stevens always bristled at being the observed, rather than the observer. He was never comfortable being commented upon. This, too, had its roots in school.

He saw another Pope, waving from a balcony, blessing the crowd with beads of a hundred colors. Everyone wore beads, beads flying to and from the balconies, beads in the street. Blue beads, green beads, obscene beads.

A man played a crazy drum solo on the bottom of two plastic buckets.

Professor Stevens was not comfortable amid this multicolored exuberance. He became a professor partly because he preferred the quiet of the library to the reckless noise of his undergraduate dorm. In silent concentration, he believed, one can most effectively be oneself. Every semester, as a professor, he requested classrooms with no windows, which were only a source of distrac-

"SIEUR GEORGE'S

tion. The outdoors are unnecessary for philosophy. And he always chose to teach standing up, feeling protected by the lectern. The less students could see him physically, while teaching, the better. Professor Stevens did have a sense of humor, but it did not bother him if, after he told a joke or an anecdote, no one in the class laughed.

He turned toward Bourbon Street and saw a man with goldilocks hair and a blue polka-dot dress. He had not shaven for a few days, this gruff goldilocks. Around his waist the man wore a white picket fence — a real, full-sized white picket fence.

Taking the icons of the culture and disrupting them, thought Stevens. *A day of social upheaval.*

"I am little Miss Sunshine," snarled this scruffy man.

A group up on a balcony threw beads to everyone who passed.

These beads represent a primitive form of commerce, an exchange of ow. A set of beads smashed into his cheek, knocking him out of his italics. Blue beads, he saw, as they dropped to the ground.

A tall girl picked them up and put them around his neck and pecked him on that same cheek. She did not understand that he was only an observer.

"I am only an ob…"

"Happy Mardi Gras!" she shrieked, and skipped down the street. Stevens had thought that she was an oversized schoolgirl, and now realized that she was a normal-sized adult in costume.

When Stevens recovered from this assault, he stepped closer to Bourbon Street. He had heard Bourbon Street in the distance, and he knew that he should approach it warily. Now he was close to it. He heard a chant: "Set them free! Set them free!"

Ah, some revelers have been arrested, he thought. *Political activism on the part of the mob. This I must see.*

As he stepped onto Bourbon Street, the crowd cheered loudly and threw beads to a balcony. Stevens looked to that balcony, saw two girls, blinked, saw the two girls more clearly, and thought, *Wow.*

Then a woman bumped him further onto Bourbon, a few more people bumped him from the side, and he found himself in the momentum of Bourbon Street. His personal space was being violated in every direction. The crowd moved him further down the street, halfway down the block, to the point where no one was controlling the movement. The people would surge in one direction, with some stumbling, hopping to one foot to maintain balance, then surge the other way. This tidal surge of human movement carried Stevens along with the crowd.

At one point the surge came to a stop; perhaps the street was too full for the crowd to continue in any direction. Stevens found himself unable to move, pressed uncomfortably close to a stranger, face to face, nearly chest to chest. Stevens' compact belly was the only barrier between them. The man was clean cut, black, with a nicely trimmed moustache. He had very clear skin. Even from here, Stevens could see no blemishes. They were pressed together, almost breathing on each other. Stevens had never been so close to a black man. His arms were awkwardly shoved into his sides by the surrounding people. He would have been more comfortable if he could have put his arms around this man; that would have been a more natural position for his awkward arms.

The man spoke, smiled, "I would move if I could."

A thought moved from Stevens' arms to his brain, and he really wanted to hug this man. There was something about that smile — a sign of camaraderie within this faceless mob. Together, as a team, they could embrace and push their way through the crowd, finding strength in unity and dancing their way to safety.

Instead the crowd moved, sending Stevens and the black man in opposite directions, never to consummate that embrace. Someone slopped a cup of beer onto Stevens' jacket. Then he was squeezed between two or three gigantic people, squeezed harder, and he popped out onto the sidewalk.

There he could breathe. He leaned on a pole supporting a balcony, breathing. Soon he saw that almost all of the crowd in the street was facing his way, staring at the balcony above him.

As he caught his breath, he began to hear them chanting, yelling, shouting toward whoever stood on that balcony. The crowd was primarily male. One male was offering a ridiculously large set of beads to someone above, more like a necklace of Christmas ornaments, but larger. The intent anticipation of all those male eyes caught Stevens' attention.

Something occurred above him, and the crowd erupted in celebration. The air was filled with flying beads, landing on, near and around that balcony; the man with the ornament beads hurled them high above Stevens, pointing to the intended recipient. The men smiled, roared, laughed, looked at each other.

I must see what is creating this commotion, thought Stevens, and for the first time in his life, he decided to join the crowd.

So Professor Stevens stepped from the sidewalk and felt his left shoe become submerged in a thick puddle by the curb. His shoe was stuck, his sock was soaked. He looked and saw that this putrid puddle was purplish black, with a trickle of greenish-gray. It appeared to be composed of mud, beer, some water, no, no, no — do not think about the composition of this puddle.

He pulled his foot free with a suction sound — thwuck! — and stepped with a soggy foot into the crowd. He felt the momentum and allowed himself to be carried further down the block. His legs were doing most of the work, with no need for help from the head.

He surged through a large group of girls, or was it a group of large girls, he could not tell as he entered an intersection, stepped to the side and found breathing room.

He felt a February breeze over his balding head. My hat, he thought, and scanned that impossible crowd for a glimpse of tweed.

"Are you with us?" a young woman glimmered up to him.

"Yes, yes," he replied, as if he was being saved.

She was dressed as an angel, with a long white gown, surprisingly transparent in some areas, golden wings and, um, yes it is, small devil horns. Stevens was usually not a fan of incongruity, but there was something enchanting about this angel. Those horns were very realistic, poking proudly though her brown hair.

"Let's go," she said, and Stevens was once again part of a crowd.

"Ooomph, ah," he replied and restarted down the street, his one wet foot slogging along.

They were in a group of about fifteen people, headed down some street off of Bourbon. A man was standing at the corner holding a very large cross, and he handed a small pamphlet to Stevens. The pamphlet told him that all of this was a sin.

A man dressed as Peter Pan asked, "How do you know Sarah and Joe?"

"You need more beads," the angel woman glimmered — that was the only word for it — as she took off some of her own beads and draped them over Stevens. "Happy Mardi Gras!" and she pecked him on the cheek.

"She loves everybody right now," said Pan. Something about this Pan was disturbing to Stevens, perhaps those green tights. Stevens tried to avoid that man altogether.

They turned into a courtyard, to the side of a very large house. Then the doors opened, food came out, drinks poured, music played. In one moment, the party was in full swing.

"You need a shot of this," said another woman, shoving a glass of clear liquid into his hand. About six people were already holding a glass of this liquid. Someone said something — drowned out by the music — and Stevens found that his own arm was caught up in the Mardi Gras momentum. He had no desire for this drink, but his arm did, and the drink lifted to his lips and slipped right in. His hand was guilty as well.

The drink burned pleasantly and coated his stomach in a way that reminded him of that angelic devil.

"I love your hat," said the glimmering devil girl.

"Huh?" he said, and reached to his head. There he found a conical stocking cap, purple, gold and green striped, with a puffy gold tassel at the tip.

"This is not …"

"That's comical," she said.

"Conical," he corrected.

"Have another," and she poured the clear liquid into his glass. The arm immediately lifted it to his lips. It was as if his body, led by his arm, was taking this chance to rebel against the brain. This was an insurgency.

"Someone's thirsty!"

With two drinks of this clear liquid, he had forgotten his soggy shoe. There were more drinks, more music, loud conversations, more costumes and faces, more laughter. Stevens did not realize that he stood in one spot the entire time. His feet did not move. He also did not realize — or did not observe — that he was having a wonderful time.

"Have you had any king cake this year? Here. Jenny already bit the baby."

A woman looking like Raggedy Ann held up a small plastic baby, dotted with frosting.

Stevens was unable to place this in his anthropological landscape. In fact, at this point, Stevens' only thought was, *Hmm, frosted baby.*

Some more people seemed to be speaking to him. They seemed to be inviting him to come along somewhere, but he could not hear a word because his head was overwhelmed by a tuba. He was standing much too close to the large speakers playing Mardi Gras music, and he had been there the entire time. The music reverberated in his besieged brain.

He followed these people out of the courtyard.

A man continued to talk to him as they walked. He was dressed in a blue suit and a red tie, and he had very slicked hair, perfectly parted, and he talked and talked. Stevens could not tell if this man was in costume. The man had an intent expression as he talked, looking straight into Stevens' eyes, adding emphasis with his hands. Stevens' brain was under control of that liquid, the siege had been successful, and he did not hear a word the man said. His head still felt as though it was inside of a tuba, but the tuba was no longer playing.

The man talked and talked. Stevens was not really concerned with what this man was saying. He was much more concerned with the question of whether or not this man was in costume. Something about his head seemed to be plastic. The lines on his face as he talked and talked seemed to indicate a mask.

"Professor Steven!"

He turned to this new voice and saw a vision in green. Bright green butterfly wings, lime green leggings, a striped top of multiple greens, even a green face. This vision said, "Professor Steven, I never thought I would see you here!"

"My name is Stevens. In school they called me uneven Stevens. Then they would knock me down."

"I was in your class, last semester, front row, ten o'clock! … Steeevens, your name makes me smile."

He was certain that he had never seen this much green in a classroom, and he said, "Do you like my comical hat?"

"You don't have a hat on."

He reached to his head, found it hatless, and said, "Hmm."

"Bye, have fun, happy Mardi Gras!" She placed a set of green beads around his neck and disappeared down the street as though some invisible force was tugging her.

The sound of laughter seemed to be everywhere. Stevens looked around the street and realized that he had lost his group. They may have been right nearby, but he could not remember what any of them looked like. He did a double take at a woman wearing paint in place of a top.

Hmm, he thought.

The parade was only a block away, on Canal Street. There, crowds of people lined both sides of the wide street. He did not want to immerse himself in yet another crowd, so he stood back, by a building.

A young woman with an oversized pacifier passed by.

With his head in this new state, the entire scene seemed

like an odd dream, with unusual exaggerations. But he did not contemplate the possible significance of that pacifier. His mind was more willing to accept, more willing to live without answering each intrigue. More willing to accept the idea of intrigue.

The first float arrived, or perhaps they had been passing the entire time and only now did Stevens see one. He was stunned by the size. This enormous float — two or three truck lengths — had its own band, many masked people throwing beads, entire bags of beads, cups, coins, trinkets, from two or three levels — blink, focus — just two, two levels. The mob jumped and reached and fought for every item, sometimes tugging a string of beads apart, little beads falling along the sidewalk. Plastic cups bounced off of fingertips, falling to the unclean street, where people picked them up as though they were precious. A frisbee hit just over his head, as if it had been aimed.

A young woman tugged at his sleeve and said, "Put me on your shoulders." Before he could respond, she was climbing Stevens like a tree. She pulled and stepped on his limbs.

With his head, this girl, and the chaos of the street, Stevens began to lose his sense of motion. The girl was almost to his shoulders. Stevens staggered forward, the girl clutched at his collar, prying her strong little fingers into his neck. He bumped into a group of people, knocking someone over, unable to control his momentum. Then he tripped on the sidewalk, fell to his knees and sent the girl toppling over his head into the street.

Then there is a blank.

Perhaps Stevens hit his head, or perhaps the mysterious liquid momentarily blacked out his brain — hint: he did not hit his head — but the next thing he knew he was walking, stumbling through the French Quarter, far away from the parade.

There he went, a man who did not participate in Mardi Gras. Mardi Gras happened to him.

He practically knocked down the Cowardly Lion — The same one? Could there be two? — stumbled through a corner filled with skin and sweat and hair and cross-dressed men — saw another Pope — stumbled for a couple of more blocks, then found himself on the outskirts of the Quarter.

The sounds of laughter, music, cheering came from every direction, but distantly. On this block there was, for the moment, no one except for Stevens. He stood there, with a wet left foot, a beer-stained jacket, an aching back and a hatless head. There were also those beads, his trinkets of victory.

His brain came back slowly, like a deposed leader returning to power: chastened, humbled, but still worthy of the throne.

So much more than social upheaval, he thought. Then he remembered his bus stop.

Only a few blocks away he found that bus stop, and he slumped onto the curb. He hung his head, and the beads swung down from his tired neck. He looked at his watch, licked his finger and smeared away the beer stain. He saw the time and thought, *Next year I will stay longer. But at least I have spent one hour.*

When the bus arrived, he stepped on, and once again heard the sound of laughter in the background. *Next year,* he thought, *I will come back to that laughter.*

*

Acknowledgments.

This book was written and designed during three months in the fall of 2005. On September 1, three days after Katrina devastated the Gulf Coast region, we decided that we had to turn our attention from Asia, where Chin Music Press is generally focused, and to New Orleans. What was happening to friends and family — and to the nation — was just too stunning. On November 28, eighty-nine days later, the book was at the printers. In that short time span, we went through two distinct phases.

In phase one, we worked like a newsroom. We monitored the news as it broke, contacted writers, whose lives were in disarray as they took refuge in other cities and towns, and asked them to write for us. We told them that we had very little money, and this was just our second book. They responded beyond our wildest dreams, and we want to thank them very much for that. They wrote their stories while sleeping on friends' couches and wondering about their neighbors, their homes. They did their edits in between consultations with insurance assessors. They were wonderful to work with, and they reaffirmed our belief that, just beneath the mainstream media's constant and numbing white noise, American eloquence and good humor is alive and well.

The second phase of this project had us working like historians. As we sifted through news reports, essays and other writings on New Orleans, we came across two books we'd like to single out as being exceptionally helpful. The first is *The World from Jackson Square*, a compilation of writings on New Orleans published in 1948 by Farrar, Straus and Co. and edited by Etolia S. Basso. This book provided us with many illuminating early takes on New Orleans, some of which are included here. The second book, which designer Craig Mod found in the library of Waseda University in Tokyo, is the *Historical Sketch Book and Guide to New Orleans*, published in 1885. Lafcadio Hearn contributed to the volume and provided us a direct link between the subject of our first book, Japan, and New Orleans. The engravings in this volume were taken from this book as were some of the song lyrics.

When we founded Chin Music Press in 2002, we wanted to make books that would be entertaining today and revealing a hundred years from now. These books that I have just mentioned fit that description nicely, and we thank the publishers, editors, writers, illustrators, designers, printers and others involved in the process for making the effort.

— Bruce Rutledge

TYPOGRAPHIC PROPORTIONS OF
ONE *DO YOU KNOW* GUMBO

0.7%	Waters Titling Pro
2%	Fedra Serif Display
97%	Minion Pro
0.15%	Fedra Sans
0.15%	Linotext

(Yes, that is an *italic* small caps up there!)

THE OAKS — Maurice Les

The Famous New Orleans Duelling Ground